Letts

KEY IDEAS

Key Stage 3

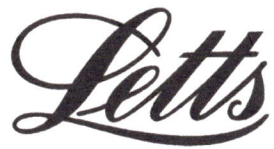

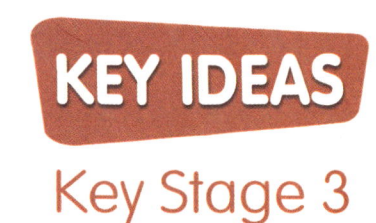

Forces

Terry Hudson and Ray Oliver

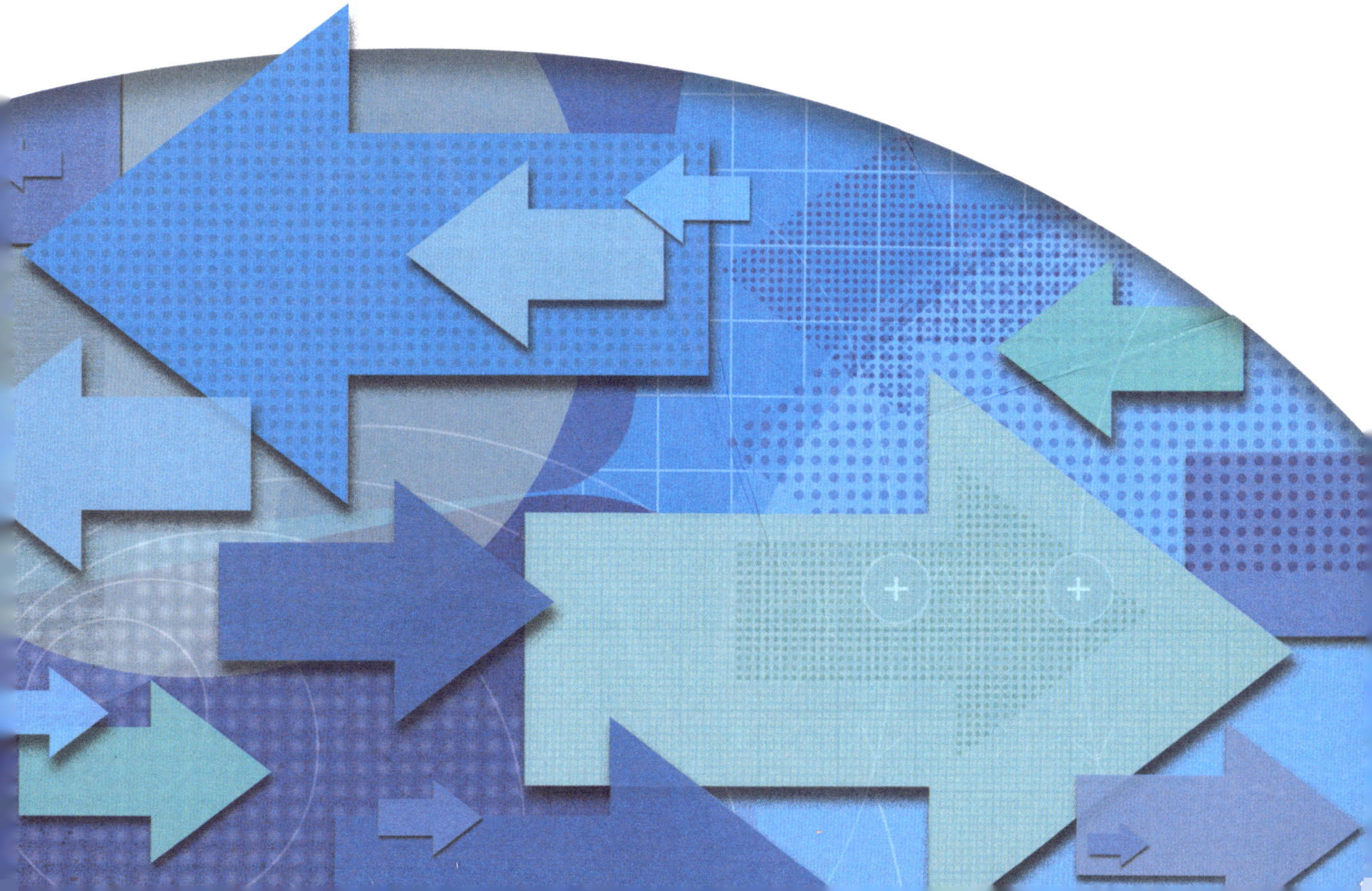

Framework objectives matched to material in this book

Teaching objective	Related chapters
Y7 F1	What are forces? 2 Balanced forces, 6
Y7 F2	Forces and movement, 10
Y7 F3	Forces and movement, 10
Y7 F4	Forces and movement, 10
Y7 F5	Mass and weight, 15
Y7 F6	Friction, 30
Y7 SE1	Balanced forces, 6 On the turn, 57
Y7 SE2	Balanced forces, 6 On the turn, 57
Y7 SE3	Forces and movement, 10
Y7 SE4	Forces and movement, 10 Science and the Martians, 25
Y7 SE5	Mass and weight, 15
Y7 SE6	Friction, 30
Y8 F1	Magnetic attraction, 42
Y8 F2	Magnetic fields, 47
Y8 F3	Electromagnets, 52

Teaching objective	Related chapters
Y8 SE1	Magnetic attraction, 42 Magnetic fields, 47
Y8 SE2	Magnetic fields, 47
Y8 SE3	Electromagnets, 52
Y9 F1	Streamlining, 36
Y9 F2	On the turn, 57
Y9 F3	Under pressure, 62 Pressure in liquids and gases, 67 Using pressure, 73
Y9 F4	Gravity extra, 19 Science and the Martians, 25
Y9 SE1	Friction, 30 Streamlining, 36
Y9 SE2	On the turn, 57
Y9 SE3	Under pressure, 62 Pressure in liquids and gases, 67 Using pressure, 73
Y9 SE4	Gravity extra, 19 Science and the Martians, 25

Contents

How to use this book

Key Ideas: *Forces* can be used as enrichment material to motivate and enthuse students following any KS3 Science course.

The 15 chapters of stimulating, cross-curricular scientific accounts and activities provide up-to-the-minute information on subjects of general topical and historical interest such as asteroid impacts, looking for evidence of life on Mars, the design of submarines, and crash dummies.

Each chapter consists of: an introduction; texts and activities; a review; and a summary. The activities cover a range of learning styles and can be used as class or group assignments, or enrichment exercises for individual pupils. To help you select material for lessons covering particular topics and skills, the grid on the facing page links Framework objectives with the relevant chapters. In the grid:

- F = Forces
- SE = Scientific Enquiry Sc1
- Objectives are numbered consecutively, following the same order as the Framework for Teaching Science.

Answers to the closed questions in the activities are on pages 79–80, and key words in the text are defined in an index and glossary on pages 81–84.

Key to coloured panels in the chapters

- lab experiments and web search activities
- written and group discussion activities
- research, evidence and scientific developments boxes
- interesting facts boxes

Key to symbols in activities boxes

- lab activity
- hazard that may be encountered during an experiment
- literacy activity
- web search activity
- Sc1 practice activity
- numeracy activity
- ICT activity, e.g. PowerPoint

What are forces?

Introduction

In this chapter we look at some different types of forces and their effects.

- Forces are pushes and pulls.
- A force can change the speed, direction and shape of an object.
- The greater the force the greater the effect it has.
- Gravitational force pulls everything down towards the Earth.
- Contact force comes when two objects collide.
- Frictional force can slow down or stop a thing that is moving.
- We can measure forces using a newtonmeter.

Think back to work you have done on forces. Write down some examples of forces you have studied. Compare your list with a partner and prepare to discuss your ideas with the rest of the class.

 A force is a push or a pull: pushing and pulling forces can have different causes. There are also turning or twisting forces.

- Any object has gravitational force due to its mass: the bigger the mass, the bigger the gravitational force of the object.
- The gravitational force of the Earth (which has a huge mass) pulls everything down towards it. A person climbing a ladder must work to overcome Earth's force of gravity. If the person slips, because of the gravitational force, they could fall to the ground and be injured.
- Contact force comes when two objects collide. This happens for example when two cars crash or when two people collide.
- Frictional force can slow down or stop an object that is moving. Slippery surfaces such as wet roads and polished floors have low friction. Surfaces that grip, such as the special rubber on racing car tyres and climbing boots, have high friction.

1 With a partner, look back at the examples of forces that you listed at the beginning of this unit. Decide whether each one is an example of a gravitational force, a contact force or a frictional force.

Crash dummies

Contact forces that occur when objects collide can:

- change the shape of an object,
- change the direction of a moving object,
- change the speed of an object, or start it moving or stop it.

Nowhere are these effects more clearly seen than in crash tests. To test the safety of cars and devices such as seat belts, scientists deliberately crash cars and examine the results. It would be dangerous for people to drive test cars, so models called crash dummies are used instead. Research has helped us to understand that in a crash there are three main effects:

- The car collides with another car or with an object such as a wall, and is rapidly slowed down and damaged.
- The driver and any passengers collide with parts of the car.
- Their internal organs collide inside their bodies.

Therefore, after the crash all the objects (which had been moving) are now stationary. In a dramatic way, the contact force has changed their speed to zero, and the shape of some objects has changed as well.

In a high-speed crash between two cars, the metal parts of the cars are crushed and bent. The force involved in the impact can move the steering wheel back a long way and injure the driver. This is why there are speed limits on roads and why drivers must be trained and need to remain alert. If an accident does happen, there are a number of safety features built into modern cars to minimise damage to the driver and passengers. These include:

- Crumple zones – the front of the car is designed to buckle up and absorb the energy of the collision. At just 40 kph, the front of a car will be crushed shorter by about 60 cm.
- Seat belts – these stop the driver and passengers from being thrown about in a crash. In a 40 kph crash, a small baby could collide with another object with a force of over 130 kg.
- Airbags – these inflate and cushion the driver and passengers from hard parts of the car.

A crash between two cars may not be head-on: instead, there could be a sideways collision. In that case, the contact forces may cause both cars to change direction before they come to a halt. The same sort of thing can happen when you kick a ball to another player. The ball changes direction when the other player provides a force by kicking it.

Crash tests are used to check that safety features in cars are able to protect the driver and passengers during a collision.

2 In this experiment you will investigate head-on car collisions.

Sc1 This is what you need:
- wooden ramp
- pile of books
- 2 toy cars
- modelling clay or similar
- metre ruler

This is what you do:

1 Set up the wood, raised up on one book to make a shallow ramp

2 Place a car at the bottom of the ramp

3 Hold the other car half-way down the ramp

You are going to let go of the car on the ramp so that it runs down the ramp and hits the car at the bottom.
- Predict what will happen.

4 Carry out the collision and record your findings
- How accurate was your prediction?

5 Investigate what happens when the ramp is raised by placing it on more books

6 Now use the modelling clay to design and test crumple zones at the front of the cars
- How does your investigation give you information about car crashes?
- Write down some safety messages you would give to car drivers.

Airbags are for adults

Deaths in head-on collisions have been cut by about 30% since airbags were first introduced in the 1980s. This is because they inflate within $\frac{1}{25}$th of a second of the collision – faster than the blink of an eye; and this happens before a person's body has time to collide with any other part of the car.

At the same time, it is important to know that airbags fly out of the dashboard at a speed of over 300 kilometres per hour, and that the huge force of a bag exploding outwards could cause serious injury to a young child or a baby. So they should never be strapped in the car near airbags. The safest place for young children and babies is in the back seat of the car.

How do airbags work?

We have found out how quickly they inflate, but how do they do this? The answer is a simple chemical reaction. An airbag system is made up of three parts:

- The bag: It is made of a nylon material covered in talcum powder to stop it sticking together when tightly folded up.

- The sensor: This detects a change in movement. It will start inflation of the bag if the car hits an object with a contact force that is the same as hitting a wall at 16 to 24 kilometres per hour.

- The inflation system: When sodium azide (NaN_3) reacts with potassium nitrate (KNO_3), a large amount of nitrogen gas is produced – explosively and therefore with tremendous force. This fills the bag extremely rapidly.

3 Work with a partner. Design and produce a poster that encourages people to use airbags safely. Include drawings that show how an airbag inflates, and the force involved.

Measuring forces

A spring balance is an instrument that measures forces. When you drop a ball it falls to the earth, because of a force called gravity. When the ball is fixed to a spring it will still try to fall to earth, but the spring stops it and it stretches. The greater the force (depending on the mass of the ball), the more the spring will stretch.

The inventor of the spring balance was Robert Hooke (1635–1702) and he discovered that the stretch of a spring is directly proportional to the force acting on it, so, if the mass of the ball doubles, the stretch also doubles. This is Hooke's law.

We measure forces in units called newtons (named after Sir Isaac Newton, famous for his discoveries about gravity). A mass of 1 kg gives a force of 9.8 newtons, and this can be seen on the scale of a spring balance called a newtonmeter. Newtonmeters are convenient for measuring forces up to 100 newtons.

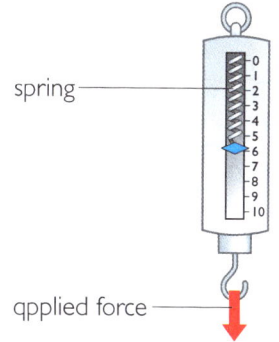

spring

applied force

A newtonmeter.

4 Work with a partner. Carry out an internet search to find out about the work of Robert Hooke:
- What other scientific discoveries did he make?
- What are some of the uses of the spring balance?
- Write a short article about Robert Hooke that shows his importance to science.

Review

Work in a group. Select one person to read out the questions and then discuss the answers. Prepare to share your ideas with other groups.

- List three examples of forces.
- What are the three possible effects that a force can have on an object?
- Describe some of the forces seen in car collisions.
- Why do seat belts and airbags save lives?
- What is the unit used to measure forces?
- Name a piece of equipment that can be used to measure forces.
- List two discoveries of Robert Hooke.

Chapter summary

In this chapter you have found out that:

- Forces can change the shape, speed and direction of an object.
- Car crashes involve collision forces that can kill or injure the driver and passengers, but seat belts and airbags can reduce injuries.
- The crumple zone of a car absorbs the force of an impact.
- Airbags expand with tremendous force.
- Forces are measured in units called newtons, named after Sir Isaac Newton.
- A newtonmeter is used to measure forces.

Balanced forces

Introduction

In this chapter we look at how we can identify the forces on an object.

- When an object is stationary the forces on it are balanced.
- In the absence of a force, an object moves at a steady speed or remains stationary.
- Two equal and opposite forces will cancel each other out.

- When forces on an object are balanced, we say that the object is in equilibrium.
- For a building, the forces must be in equilibrium or the building would fall down.

Look around the room. List five objects that are held in place by other objects. Discuss your list with a partner and try to write down the forces on each of your objects.

 A stone placed on a table will stay there until a force acts on it. A spacecraft moving through outer space will continue at a steady speed unless a force acts on it. There is no change unless a force is applied to an object.

As you know, a force is a push or a pull. A force can give energy to an object and can make it change its shape, its direction or its speed. Forces can make objects start moving or stop them.

A bulldozer can push into an object with such force that the object moves. This is why bulldozers are used to move heavy objects. Animals also push into each other. You may have seen film of bull elephants pushing into each other as they fight to see who is the number one male. At times, one bull elephant pushes the other bull backwards. Sometimes they push with equal force and are locked in place – not moving in any direction. When this happens, we say that the forces are balanced. We use arrows to represent forces.

Arrows represent the forces exerted by the elephants.

1 With a partner, discuss some examples of objects (or animals) pushing into each other.

- Decide on one example where the forces are balanced and one example where the forces are not balanced.
- Draw sketches of your examples.
- Add arrows to your sketches to show the forces.

Tug-of-war

A well-known example of balanced forces can be seen in a tug-of-war. This time the forces on the rope are pulls. Each team heaves away and tries to pull the other team across a line. If the teams are equally strong they will pull with equal force. The teams do not move. We can say that the forces are 'balanced' or that they are 'in equilibrium'. They mean the same thing.

There are some other forces in equilibrium here: the force upwards by the ground must balance the downward force of the feet, or the team would sink into the ground.

On the pull

Not all tug-of-war teams are highly trained athletes. Many fun events are arranged for charity, but the forces are the same. The article on the right describes a tug-of-war event between members of the UK parliament, journalists and television broadcasters.

Pimms, stilettos and muscular ministers

The Backbencher reports from the annual parliamentary tug-of-war

The 16th annual parliamentary tug-of-war, in aid of Macmillan Cancer Relief, was parliament's own Ascot. Pimms was served at a reception in Westminster Abbey's surprisingly large college garden. Stilettos sank into the grass. Peers were introduced to small dogs. MPs whose inferior physiques prevented them from joining in cast mildly resentful glances at their colleagues.

Jane Asher did a fabulous job of cheering on the broadcasters' team. 'Can I just say how suitably dressed you are for a tug-of-war, Jane,' Radio 2 presenter Don Maclean told her as she picked her way on to the field. The Backbencher hates to admit it, but the broadcasters were in fine condition.

With the help of inspired cheerleading from Felicity Kendal-Rudman, the bulkier press corps were soon victorious.

The Guardian

---

2 Work on your own to answer these questions.

a Why do larger people tend to do better in a tug-of-war than smaller people?

b Draw a diagram of a tug-of-war between two equally strong teams, each with 8 tuggers.

c Draw in force arrows to show how the forces are balanced.

d What would happen if an extra tugger joined one team?

e Write a short article for a newspaper to describe the tug-of-war.

Bridges

Bridges have to be carefully designed. A bridge has to support its own weight as well as the weight of traffic or trains being pulled down by gravity. These downward forces have to be balanced by upward forces, and the upward forces are produced by the supports of the bridge. If the bridge forms an arch, the curve of the arch transfers the downward forces sideways to the supports. In a suspension bridge, the downward forces are balanced by upward forces exerted by the towers and the cables that suspend the roadway.

Buildings and balanced forces

The fact that a building does not collapse means that the forces must be balanced. Architects make sure that the downward forces from the weight of the roof, floors and walls are balanced by upward forces applied by the lower sections of the walls and the foundations.

Lean-to

The Leaning Tower of Pisa is a good example of what happens if the foundations cannot support the weight of a building. It began to lean almost as soon as building started in 1173. A great deal of money has been spent to improve the foundations, balance the forces on the building and make sure that it does not fall over.

3 You are going to make a bridge out of spaghetti.

Work in a group. You will be competing against other groups to build a bridge. The winning bridge will be the one that spans a 20 cm gap and holds the greatest mass in the middle before it breaks.

Each group will need:
- 20 pieces of dry spaghetti
- glue gun
- access to assorted masses
- 2 wooden blocks 20 cm × 20 cm × 20 cm

⚠️ Careful: the glue will be hot.

This is what you do:

1 Design a bridge that spans the 20 cm gap between the two wooden blocks

2 Build your bridge. Use as many of the pieces of spaghetti as you feel are necessary to support the masses when your bridge is tested. Remember: it must support the mass exactly in the middle

3 Draw your bridge: mark the downward forces and the upward forces

4 Now test it
- In a table of results, record the masses added and their effect.
- How did you design your bridge to overcome the downward force of the mass in the middle?
- At what stage did the forces on your bridge become unbalanced?
- How would you improve your design?

Lifting objects

To carry an object, you must first lift it with an upward force that is greater than the downward force of the object due to gravity. To hold it steady, the upward force must equal the downward force due to gravity. The heavier the object, the more force you need to use to lift it. That is why only the strongest people can lift the sort of weights that Olympic weightlifters use. While the weight is above their head, and is held steady, the forces are balanced. For much lighter weights, when you carry your books across a room or help out with bags of shopping, you are also balancing forces.

4 List five examples of when you have used balanced forces to carry an object. Rank the examples, with the one needing the most force at the top. Compare your list with a partner.

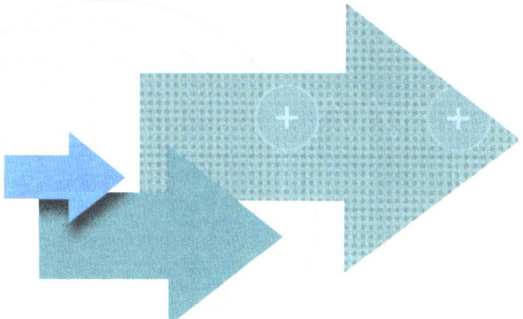

Review

Form the class into four teams. The statements below will be read out and you will have one minute to discuss and write down your group's response to each one. Each statement is either true or false. The team with the most correct responses wins.

- A book resting on a table is an example of balanced forces.
- A person holding a mirror in front of their face is an example of balanced forces.
- A bridge would collapse if the downward forces were not balanced by upward forces.
- When one tug-of-war team wins the forces must have been balanced.
- An arch bridge transfers weight to the supports at each end.
- When you sit on a chair and it doesn't collapse, the forces must be balanced.

Chapter summary

In this chapter you have found out that:
- When the forces acting on an object are equal we say that they are balanced.
- With balanced forces, the forces cancel each other out.
- An equal tug-of-war is an example of balanced forces.
- In buildings and bridges the forces must be balanced, otherwise these structures would collapse.
- To hold an object, you must balance the downward force of gravity with an upward, lifting force.

Forces and movement

Keeping moving

Once an object is moving, it will keep moving unless a force acts against it. This is best seen in space. Once on the move, a spacecraft will continue to travel through space at the same speed and in the same direction forever, without any need for a force to propel it. That is, it continues to move in the same way forever unless it hits another object, or is affected by gravity, or its rockets are fired to alter its speed or direction.

It was an Italian scientist called Galileo Galilei (1564–1642) who realised that, though an object needs a force to make it start or to make it move faster, it does not need a force to keep it moving. This idea was developed further by Sir Isaac Newton (1642–1727) who established three laws of motion.

Newton's first law – the law of inertia

If an object is not being pushed or pulled it will stay in the same place or, if it is moving, it will keep moving at the same speed and in the same direction. The greater the mass of the object, the greater is its inertia.

If you have ever been in a car when the driver slams on the brakes, you will know about Newton's first law. He called the effect 'inertia'. As the car stops abruptly, you continue to move forward. When you are in a moving car you are obviously travelling at the same speed as the car – and when the car stops, your body continues to move. It keeps moving until acted on by a force. This may be a collision with the inside of the car or with other passengers. If you are very unlucky, you may even be thrown through the windscreen. But if you have been sensible you will be stopped by a seat belt applying a force to halt your motion.

How a seat-belt works

In a car crash, it takes less than one tenth of a second for people to be slammed into the interior structure of the car. A seat belt halts your body, but if it stopped you too quickly you could be injured. Seat belts are designed to stretch slightly and absorb some of the shock of the impact in a crash. The seat belt spreads the force of the impact over the stronger parts of your body such as hips, shoulders and chest. This is why it is vital to check that seat belts are fitted properly.

1 Work in a small group to investigate inertia.

You will need:
- wooden ramp
- pile of books
- wooden block
- toy car
- small figure of a person

This is what you do:

1 Set up the wooden ramp by placing one end on a small pile of books

2 Place the wooden block at the bottom of the ramp

3 Hold the car at the top of the ramp and place the small figure, to represent the driver, in (or on) the car

4 Let the car run down the ramp and collide with the block

5 Write down your observations

6 Repeat the investigation, but alter the height of the ramp by adding more books

7 Record what happens to the driver and what happens to the block during each collision

- What do your investigations tell you about inertia?
- Write a brief report of your findings and conclusions.

The law of inertia tells us that a moving object tends to continue to move; it also tells us that an object at rest will stay at rest unless acted on by an unbalanced force. You may have watched people trying to push a broken-down car; this is a good example of inertia. They have to push very hard to get the car to start moving at all, and then they have to keep pushing to make it move faster. It is even harder to push a broken-down lorry: this is because the greater the mass of an object, the greater will be its inertia.

Inertia and party tricks

You may have seen a magician skillfully pull a table-cloth out from under cups, plates and saucers on a table. Each item has inertia and will stay at rest unless acted on by a force. A really smooth tablecloth, pulled out fast enough, will not create enough force to move the crockery.

2 Rather than smash all the dishes at home, try this variation of the same trick.

You will need:
- 50p coin
- glass tumbler
- piece of card 10 cm × 15 cm

This is what you do:

1 Place the card centred on top of the glass tumbler

2 Put the coin at the centre of the card

3 Flick the card with your finger so that it moves sideways off the beaker 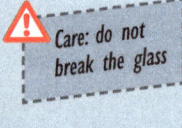 *Care: do not break the glass*

4 Record what happens to the coin

5 Repeat the investigation using smaller coins and different types of card

6 Record what happens each time

7 Write down how the magic coin and card trick uses Newton's first law.

Newton's second law

> When a force acts on an object it will start to move, change direction or slow down. The greater the force, the greater the change in motion.

We can explain Newton's second law by thinking about a spacecraft.

Earlier in this chapter we saw that a spacecraft continues to travel in the same direction and at the same speed as long as no forces are acting upon it. But what happens if we do apply a force?

When the spacecraft fires its rockets it will start to move faster: it will accelerate. A powerful rocket that provides a great deal of force will cause the spacecraft to accelerate

more than a smaller rocket would. The same thing happens on Earth as well.

Drag racing cars, built to accelerate rapidly over a short distance, have powerful engines. These provide as much force as possible. The mass of a drag racing car is kept to a minimum. If a drag racing car was very large and heavy, even the most powerful engines would not give enough acceleration.

Obviously there is a link between the mass of the object and the acceleration produced by a given force. The best combination for rapid acceleration is a large force acting on an object with a small mass. We can represent this in a mathematical way by using the formula:

Force (newtons)
$$= \text{mass (kilograms)} \times \text{acceleration (metres per second}^2)$$

We define acceleration like this:
$$\text{Acceleration} = \frac{\text{change in velocity}}{\text{time taken}}$$

Karate and Newton

Sir Isaac Newton would not have known about karate, but his second law helps to explain it. A karate expert can break blocks just by using his or her hand. A human hand has a mass of approximately 0.75 kg, so you might imagine it would be very difficult to use such a small mass to break a strong block. However, experts can use techniques that allow their total body mass to be used: together with the acceleration of their hand moving so quickly, they can generate enough force to break the block. A total body mass of 80 kg, accelerating at the speed that a karate expert can move at, can generate a force of 4000 newtons. This is easily enough to break a block of wood.

There is an illustration of Newton's second law that is even easier to understand. If you had to have a ball dropped 2 metres onto your head, would you choose a solid wooden ball or a football?

Newton's third law

To every action there is an equal and opposite reaction. This means that when you pull an object it will pull you with an equal force in the opposite direction.

A 'skeet shooter' uses a shotgun to shoot down clay discs. The discs are thrown up into the air by a machine and the skeet shooter has only a short time to aim and fire. When the shotgun is fired, the force blasts pellets out of the gun at tremendous speed. The skeet shooter feels a force in the opposite direction as the gun jerks back into their shoulder. This is called the 'recoil' and is an example of Newton's third law.

The laws of motion and bumper car physics

Bumper cars are specially designed to avoid danger to their drivers when the cars collide. There is a wide rubber bumper all round each car. The bumper's flexibility means that the cars do not stop immediately on impact. It takes time for the cars to stop completely, so reducing the forces on the drivers.

Above the cars is a wire grid which carries electricity that can be turned on and off. An insulated pole at the back of each car connects the car to the grid. Electrical energy passes to the car's motor where most of it is converted to kinetic energy (energy of movement) to drive the car. A little of the energy is wasted as heat and sparks.

When two bumper cars collide, the drivers sense a change in their motion. The cars may stop or change direction but the inertia of the drivers causes them to continue in the direction in which they were moving before colliding. The greater the speed of the cars, the greater the jolt the drivers will experience. Their movement relative to the bumper cars depends on whether the collision is head-on or sideways. What happens to the drivers also depends on their mass. A heavy driver will experience a greater change in motion than a light driver.

The effects on the driver and passengers when bumper cars are in collision show just how important it is to wear seat belts in a real car.

5 Work with a partner. Read the information about bumper cars on page 13. It contains examples of the laws of motion. List as many examples as you can, and state which of the three laws is being described.

Review

Work with a small group. Think back over the chapter to remind yourself of the three laws of motion. Then try to think of an example of an amusement park ride that demonstrates each of the three laws.

- For each example, state the law and explain how it is applied.
- How are the passengers protected from injury in any collisions?
- Finally, design a new ride that would allow the passengers to experience all three laws in one ride.

Chapter summary

- The laws of motion, which Sir Isaac Newton developed, apply in everyday life.
- Newton's first law is called the law of inertia.
- The more mass an object has, the more inertia it will have.
- Car passengers would be injured in crashes if seat belts did not control their inertia.
- Designers of drag race cars use the second law, as they know that a large force and a small mass gives the greatest acceleration.
- Newton's third law states that for every action there is an equal and opposite reaction.

Mass and weight

Introduction

In this chapter we look at the differences between mass and weight.

- The mass of an object is a measure of the amount of matter it consists of.
- Mass is measured in grams (g) or kilograms (kg).
- Weight is the force of gravity pulling the object, towards the Earth or other body.
- Weight is a force and is measured in newtons (N).
- Lots of ways have been used to measure weight throughout history.

Work with a partner. Think of examples of things that you have weighed. Write down:

- how you weighed each object;
- the name of the units you used.

Discuss how much each of the objects would weigh in space. Explain your answers.

The mass of the person in the photograph is 80 kilograms. Every atom of every substance in his body contributes to his mass. Wherever the person goes his mass will be the same.

We are pulled towards the Earth by the force of gravity – a force of attraction. The force that gravity exerts on an object's mass is called its weight. We measure weight in newtons, just as we do for other forces. We have seen that the force of the attraction depends on the mass of the objects: the greater the mass of an object, the greater the force of gravity. This means that objects with bigger masses are heavier. A mass of one kilogram on Earth has a weight of 9.8 newtons.

1 Work with a partner to calculate how many newtons each of the following objects weighs on Earth.

  a A child with a mass of 28.4 kg

  b A person with a mass of 98 kg

  c A boulder with a mass of 980 kg

2 In the article about John Minnoch, notice that the author uses kilograms as the unit of weight. You know that this isn't correct.

  a Convert all the masses that are given in the article to newtons.

  b Write a letter to the author to point out why it is wrong for Jon Minnoch's weight to be given in kilograms.

The world's heaviest man

The heaviest person in medical history was Jon Brower Minnoch (USA, 1941–83), who had suffered from obesity since childhood. He was 185 cm (6 ft 1 in) tall and weighed 17 kg (28 st) in 1963, 317 kg (50 st) in 1966, and 442 kg (69 st 9 lb) in September 1976.

In March 1978, Minnoch was admitted to University Hospital, Seattle, where Dr Robert Schwartz calculated that Minnoch must have weighed more than 635 kg (100 st), a great deal of which was water accumulation due to his heart disease.

In order to get Minnoch to University Hospital, it took a dozen firemen and a home-made stretcher to move him from his home to a ferry-boat. When he arrived at the hospital, saturated with fluid and suffering from heart failure, he was put in two beds lashed together. It took 13 people just to roll him over.

After nearly two years on a diet of 1200 calories per day, he was discharged at 216 kg (34 st) – the greatest weight loss for a human being. In October 1981, though, he had to be readmitted – after putting on over 89 kg (34 st). When he died on September 10, 1983, he weighed more than 362 kg (57 st).

From The Guinness Book of Records

Massive in size and weight

The Tsing Ma Bridge in Hong Kong is the world's longest road and rail suspension bridge: its longest span is 1.4 kilometres, and the whole bridge extends 2.2 km. It is also one of the world's heaviest bridges, made of 55 000 tonnes of steel. (A tonne is 1000 kilograms.)

Mass and weight in the Solar System

We have seen that, because of their mass, all objects have a gravitational pull on other objects. We have also looked at the relationship between mass, gravity and weight. We have seen that:

- the greater the mass of an object (such as the Earth), the greater is its gravitational pull;

- the greater the gravitational pull, the greater is the weight of another object within the region of that gravitational pull.

This means that an object on a planet of high mass has a higher *weight* than it has on a planet with a lower mass.

The bodies in the Solar System have different masses. The masses of some of the planets and the Moon are given in the table. Notice the way that very large numbers are written down. This is to make sure we do not have to write huge numbers with lots of zeros. For example:

5.97×10^{24} kg, the mass of the Earth, would otherwise be written as:
5 970 000 000 000 000 000 000 000 kg.

'5.97×10^{24}' means '5.97 multiplied by 10 exactly 24 times.'

The important thing to realise is that 10^{24} is ten times bigger than 10^{23}, and 10^{23} is ten times bigger that 10^{22}.

Object	Mass in kilograms	Mass compared to mass on Earth
Jupiter	1.89×10^{27}	318.0 times
Saturn	5.68×10^{26}	95.0
Neptune	1.02×10^{26}	17.0
Uranus	8.68×10^{25}	14.5
Earth	5.97×10^{24}	1.00
Venus	4.86×10^{24}	0.82
Mars	6.41×10^{23}	0.107
Mercury	3.30×10^{23}	0.056
Moon	7.35×10^{22}	0.16

3 A person weighs 600 newtons on Earth. Calculate how much the person would weigh on:

a the Moon

b Jupiter

c Neptune

d Mercury.

The confusion about mass and weight

As you saw in the passage from the *Guinness Book of Records*, it is easy for people to get mixed up when they talk about mass and weight. When you stand on the bathroom scales it is the gravitational pull of the Earth that pulls you down onto the scales. It is your weight that is being measured. This is a force, so your weight should be given in newtons. The problem is, most scales give a reading in kilograms. No wonder people are confused! They often use mass and weight to mean the same thing. At least you will now be able to understand the difference.

4 Work with a partner. You will need a set of bathroom scales.

This is what you do:

1 Stand on the scales and write down your weight. Remember to convert kilograms to newtons

2 Still standing on the scales, throw your arms into the air, and write down what happens to the reading on the scales

3 Let your partner repeat this experiment

• What happened to your weight as you moved up and down?

• Discuss and then write down a possible explanation

• What happened to your mass as you jumped up and down?

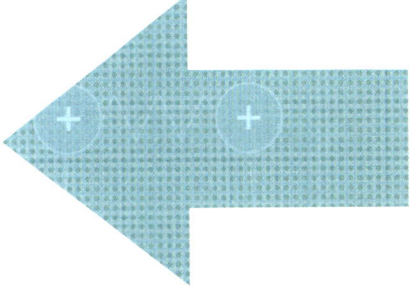

Review

Work with a partner and then prepare to share your ideas with the class.

- Design and produce a poster that could be used in supermarkets to explain to shoppers the difference between mass and weight.
- Include some easy-to-follow examples and make your poster colourful and eye-catching.

Chapter summary

In this chapter you have found out that:

- Mass is a measurement of the amount of matter that something contains.
- Weight is the measurement of the pull of gravity on an object.
- Mass is measured in kilograms and weight is measured in newtons.
- On Earth a mass of one kilogram weighs 9.8 newtons.
- The mass of an object does not change if it moves from one planet to another, but its weight does change.
- Some people are confused by mass and weight, and in everyday life mass and weight are sometimes used to mean the same thing.

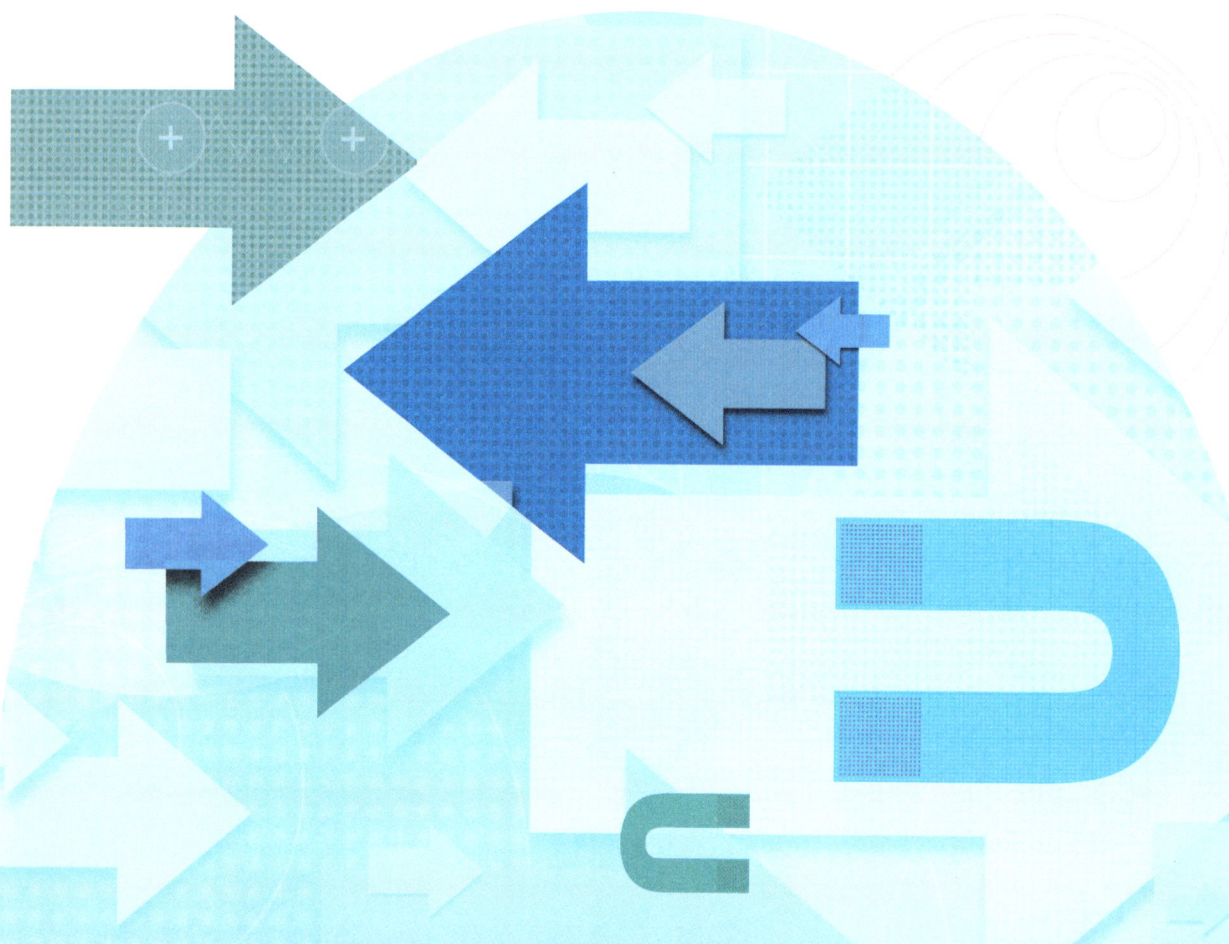

Gravity extra

Introduction

In this chapter we look at how we came to understand gravity.

- Gravity is a force of attraction.
- Everything attracts everything gravitationally.
- Large objects have a bigger gravitational pull than small ones.
- Gravity acts at a distance, even across space.
- The force of gravity depends on the distance between objects: the further away, the less the attraction.

Imagine that someone switched off gravity on Earth. How would your life change? What would be easier and what might be a problem?

The evidence

When an apple is ripe at the end of the summer, it can fall off the tree and down to the ground. People will have seen this happen for thousands of years. It took someone as bright as Isaac Newton to realise that this simple observation needed an explanation. Why doesn't the apple fall sideways or upwards when it leaves the branch?

Most of the key ideas about gravity were contained in Newton's book published in 1687. Newton said that the Earth attracted the apple by the force of gravity. This is why it fell towards the Earth. He also said that the apple attracts the Earth towards itself. Since the mass of the Earth is so much larger than the apple, the effect of the Earth moving towards the apple must be very small. The general rule is: the greater the mass, the greater the force of gravity. Wherever you stand on Earth, the force of gravity pulls you towards the Earth.

Understanding the importance of gravity.

Fatal attraction

There are big lumps of rock moving through space known as asteroids or minor planets. Some scientists believe that asteroids are the remains of another planet that broke up into pieces in the distant past. The largest asteroid known in the Solar System is called Ceres. It has a diameter of about 800 kilometres.

Many small fragments of rock head towards the Earth every day. When they hit the atmosphere they heat up and start to burn away. We call them meteors or, if they reach the Earth's surface before burning up completely, they are called meteorites.

A few years ago astronomers discovered a new asteroid which they named XF11. It is heading our way and will eventually come under the influence of the Earth's gravity. The astronomers did their calculations and worked out the time that the asteroid is due to arrive – October 2028. However, astronomers predict that there will be a near miss, expecting XF11 to come no closer than about 1 million kilometres, that is, about $2\frac{1}{2}$ times the distance of the Earth from the Moon.

Plain lunacy

The Moon is much smaller than the Earth and its mass is far less too – about one eightieth of Earth's mass. However, the Moon's gravity is still strong enough to attract asteroids. When they hit the surface they create craters. Since the Moon has no atmosphere it has no weather, so the craters do not become eroded or fill up with new rocks. Consequently we can see the whole history of asteroid impacts on the lunar surface.

Asteroids colliding with the Moon have formed its craters.

1 You are going to investigate the impacts that asteroids make.

Scl You will need:
- small plastic bottle with a top
- tray of damp sand or soil to represent the surface of a planet
- ruler

This is what you do:

1 Half fill the bottle with water and drop it from a measured height on to the sand

2 Measure the impact crater, noting its size and depth

3 Use different amounts of water in the bottle and repeat the process

- What is the connection between the mass of the 'asteroid' bottle and the size of the crater?

Siberian drama

The eastern part of Russia is called Siberia, and much of it is covered in forests. Over the forest, on 30 June 1908, there was a gigantic explosion equivalent to a 2-megatonne atomic bomb. A fireball was seen in the sky, and trees in a huge area were flattened, but no crater and no traces of the object from space were ever found. Some people think the event was caused by a meteorite which was heated by the atmosphere, broke up and exploded.

When meteorites are attracted by the Earth's gravity, some of their energy of movement, called kinetic energy, is converted into heat. Just as bicycle brakes get hot as a cyclist slows down rapidly, so meteorites heat up in the atmosphere: the air acts as a brake. The meteorites may become incandescent and start to glow brightly. We call them shooting stars. The kinetic energy of meteorites can produce enough force on impact to flatten trees and form deep craters.

The Arizona crater is over 1 kilometre wide. The meteor that formed it is thought to have had a mass of about 300 000 tonnes and been 50 metres wide.

2 Working with a partner, choose one of the following topics to carry out research on the internet.

- asteroids and meteors
- Tunguska event, 1908
- Arizona meteor crater
- Giuseppe Piazzi, discoverer of the first asteroid in 1801

3 With a partner, view this website, which gives a calendar of meteor showers: **http://comets.amsmeteors.org/meteors/calendar.html**

Prepare a short PowerPoint presentation of your findings.

Comets are slowly shrinking

Every ten years or so, bright objects with long shining tails are seen in the night sky and at twilight. These are comets and they travel round the Sun, held in eternal orbit by the Sun's gravitational force. The same force holds the planets in their orbits too.

Comets are sometimes described as dirty snowballs because, we believe, many are made of ice and dust. The ice may be of water, or it could be solid carbon dioxide since, at the very low temperatures of outer space, carbon dioxide gas freezes to a solid. When a comet approaches the Sun, its heat energy vaporises some of the solid ice and this streams out, forming a tail of gas. The tail can stretch millions of kilometres away from the comet. Whichever direction the comet is moving in, the force of the solar wind sweeps the comet's tail in the direction away from the Sun.

Comet Hale-Bopp seen in 1976. The dark blue tail is made up of gas particles that glow as they collide with high-energy particles from the Sun, while dust particles form the pale blue tail.

Halley's Comet

The most famous comet of all is named after the British astronomer Edmond Halley (1656–1742). He was at school in London and dropped out of Oxford University in 1676 without taking his degree. In 1705 he published a book in Latin called *A Synopsis of the Astronomy of Comets* which made his reputation and he went on to become Astronomer Royal.

Halley realised that reports of comets in the sky in 1531, 1607 and 1682 were all about the same comet which was returning at regular intervals. Halley's comet travels far away from the Sun before being drawn back again by the force of the Sun's gravity. The strength of gravitational attraction gets less as the distance between objects increases. This applies to all objects, including planets and stars. So, even at the comet's furthest point from the Sun, the Sun's gravitational attraction is enough to make it swing round and start its return journey.

Halley's comet returns about every 76 years and was last seen clearly from Earth in 1986.

4 Write answers to the questions below, then compare them with a partner.

a Why do comets orbit endlessly around the Sun instead of disappearing into space?

b Work out when Halley's comet will next be seen clearly from Earth.

5 To make a model comet, you will need:
- hair drier or fan heater to represent the solar wind
- threads of cotton or wool stuck to a golf ball, the comet

This is what you do:

1 Set up the fan blowing across a large table

2 Bring the model comet gradually closer to the fan, and note the effect on the tail

3 The solar wind is a stream of high-energy particles coming out from all points of the surface of the Sun. Rotate the fan to produce this effect as the comet travels round it

a In real comets, why does the tail change size as the comet approaches the Sun?

b Explain why the tail points away from the Sun.

Comet mystery

NASA has undertaken a mission, called the Deep Impact Mission. The aim is to blast open a comet to find out what is inside. NASA has sent a rocket into space that will fire a projectile into Comet Tempel 1. This will create a crater bigger than the Colosseum, a large ancient amphitheatre in Rome. Scientists hope that the crater will reveal material and debris beneath the comet's surface. The substances should be unaltered since the birth of the Solar System, providing vital information on how the Sun and planets were formed.

Galileo's big problem

Galileo was an Italian astronomer (1564–1642) whose observations changed the way we think about the universe. He was born in the city of Pisa, with the famous leaning tower. He designed and built a telescope and was one of the first people to study the sky systematically.

At this time, people believed that the Earth was the centre of everything. All the planets and the Sun were supposed to be in orbit around the Earth. This was called the 'geocentric' system, meaning 'with the Earth in the middle'.

Galileo's observations of the planet Jupiter on 7 January 1610 showed that this idea was nonsense. He saw through his telescope that there were three small bright stars, two to the east of Jupiter and one to the west. They seemed to be in a straight line. A day later, he noticed something very odd. These stars had moved. They were still in a line but now all of them were to the west of Jupiter. At that time, people believed that the stars were in fixed positions in the sky. Either this idea was wrong or the 'moving stars' near Jupiter were not stars. Over the next few nights, he again observed them changing position. Galileo realised that the bright objects were not stars at all, but were moons in orbit round the planet Jupiter.

If Jupiter could have moons orbiting round it, then the planets could be in orbit round the Sun, not round the Earth. This confirmed the theory first proposed by Copernicus (1473–1543). The religious leaders in Italy refused to believe Galileo's evidence and insisted that he gave up his ideas. He was exiled to his villa at Arcetri and was not allowed to publish his ideas any more.

6 Work with a partner to answer these questions. When you have finished, compare notes with another group.

  a What is meant by a geocentric system?

  b What was the importance of the 'moving stars' observed by Galileo?

Review

Write each question on a card. Shuffle the cards and give one to each group.
Groups have five minutes to prepare an answer, and will then explain it to the class.

  ◖ Why might asteroids be a danger to life on Earth?

  ◖ How might the extinction of the dinosaurs be connected with space?

  ◖ What do you know about comets?

  ◖ How did Galileo change the way we think about the Sun and planets?

Chapter summary

In this chapter you have found out that:

◖ Gravity is a force of attraction between all objects.

◖ Gravity acts across space and holds planets and comets in orbit.

◖ The force of gravity depends on the masses of the objects and the distance between them.

◖ Galileo's observations of the moons of Jupiter showed that objects can be in orbit around bodies other than the Earth. He showed that the geocentric theory was wrong.

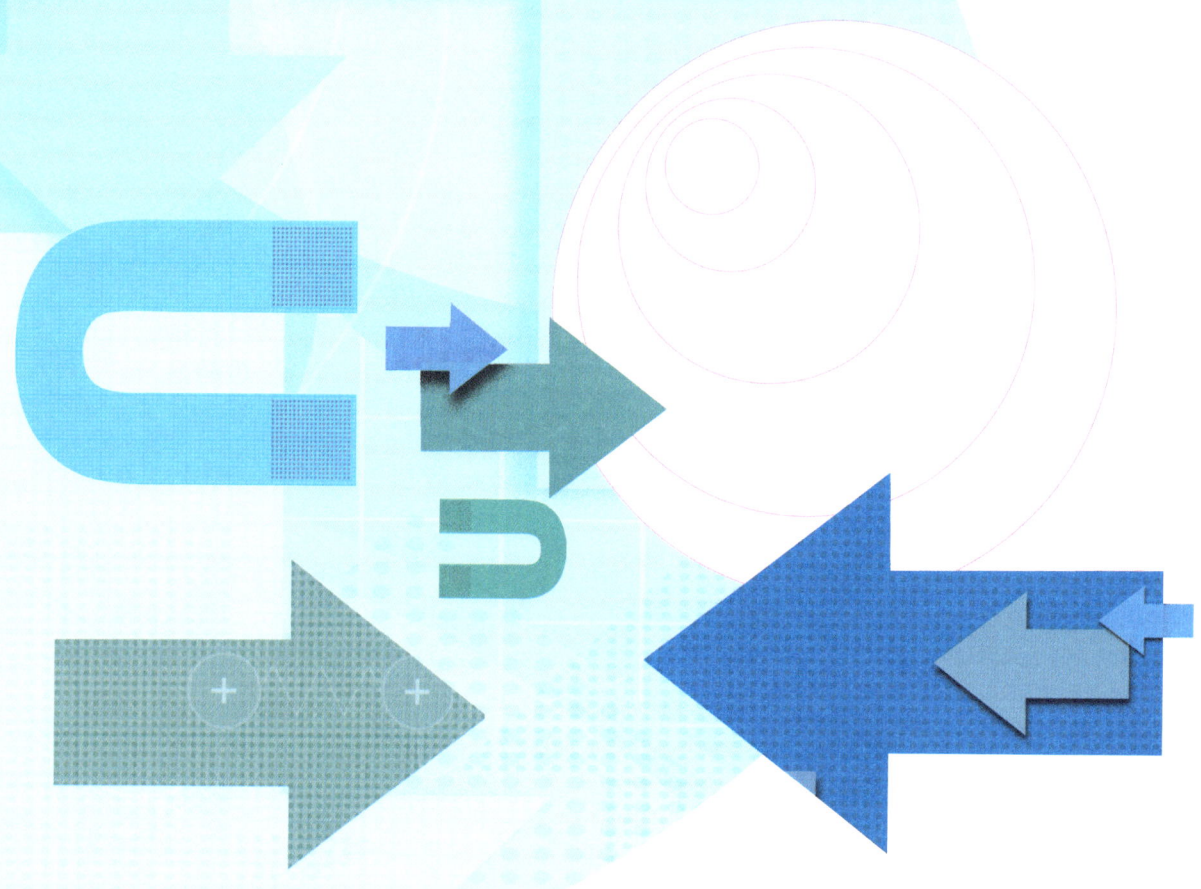

Science and the Martians

Introduction

In this chapter we look at the planet Mars.

- Mars has been important in mythology as the God of War.
- Mars moves in a mysterious way in the sky.
- The presence of 'canals' on Mars once made people think that Martians might exist there.
- Working out how to travel to Mars is complicated.
- Mars has the largest known volcano in the Solar System.

Do you believe that there may be life on other planets?

Mythological Mars

Both the Ancient Greeks and the Romans had a God of War. To the Greeks he was Ares, but the Roman god was called Mars. This is how we get the term martial arts, connected with fighting. Ares and Aphrodite, the goddess of love, had two sons whom they named Demos and Phobos. These are the names given to the moons of the planet Mars. It seems likely that these moons are asteroids, captured and held by the gravitational attraction of Mars.

Mars, the red planet.

Mars moves strangely

People have studied the movements of Mars throughout history. Its distinctive red colour makes it easy to locate in the night sky. One thing about Mars that used to be a mystery is that its size and its brightness seem to vary quite a lot. As with all the planets, the orbit of Mars is not circular – it is an ellipse. Also, Mars and Earth orbit at different speeds. Sometimes Mars gets very close to the Earth, but at other times it is much further away. This explains why the appearance of Mars varies.

When the Earth, Sun and Mars are all in a line, with the Earth in the middle, we say that Mars is 'in opposition'. An opposition of Mars occurs about every two years, and the distances of Mars from the Earth in opposition vary from 56 to 97 million kilometres.

Mysterious planet

When early astronomers began to record the movements of the red planet, they noticed something very strange. Mars sometimes seemed stationary for a few days or even to move backwards when viewed against the stars. We call this the 'retrograde motion' of the planet. It happens because the Earth is itself moving as well. (It also moves faster in its orbit than Mars.) We are not watching Mars from a fixed platform but as if from a moving train. Look at the diagram for the positions of Mars, viewed from Earth, from days 1 to 7.

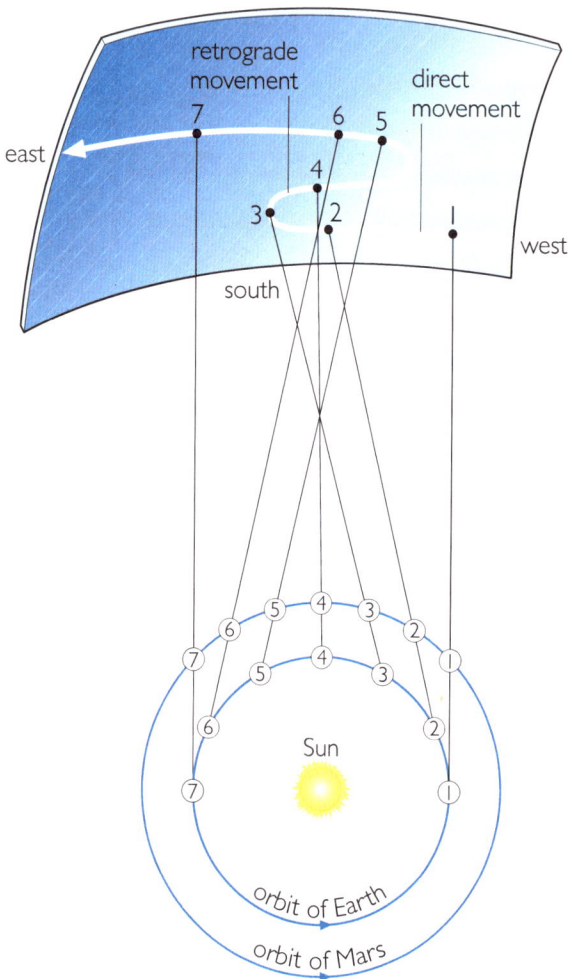

The retrograde motion of Mars as it appears from Earth. (For simplicity, the orbits are drawn as circles.)

1 Work with a partner to answer these questions. When you finish, explain your answers to another group.

a What is unusual about the movement of Mars as it appears from Earth?

b Using the diagram, describe the positions of Mars on days 1 to 7.

c How do these observations support the theory that the planets orbit the Sun rather than orbiting the Earth?

2 You are going to construct a model to demonstrate the orbits of Earth and Mars.

You will need:
- large piece of paper, ruler, pencil
- string and pin
- three round objects to represent Sun, Earth and Mars

This is what you do:

1 Place the Sun in the centre of the paper and draw round it

2 Using the pin, pencil and string, draw two large circles round the Sun to represent the orbits of Earth and Mars

3 Gradually move the model Earth and Mars so that the Earth overtakes Mars on the inside orbit

4 At intervals, draw lines between the planets, extending them out as in the diagram of retrograde motion.

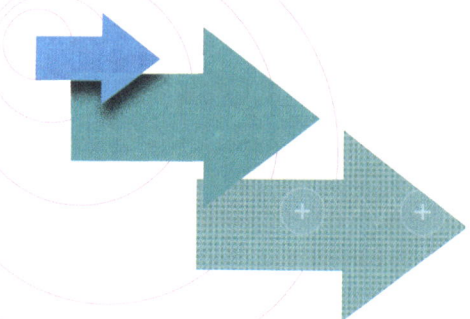

What about Martians?

Galileo observed the movements of Mars in 1610. From then on, astronomers have wondered about the possibility of life on the red planet. The surface of Mars has dark patches that people believed were seas. At the north and south Martian poles there are ice caps which change size according to the seasons. This ice may be solid carbon dioxide rather than water ice as on Earth. Observers also noticed markings on Mars that they believed were clouds.

A great sensation was caused by a report in 1877 by the Italian astronomer Giovanni Schiaparelli. He had been studying the surface features of Mars and was convinced he could see some mysterious lines or grooves running across the landscape. His report, in Italian, described these unidentified lines as 'canali'. When this was translated into English, the newspapers claimed that he had discovered a system of canals on Mars, and that they must have been built by Martians.

Unfortunately it all turned out to be an illusion. Now that spacecraft have photographed the surface of Mars, it is clear that they were not canals at all but features formed naturally.

Vast canyons on the surface of Mars.

Looking for evidence of life on Mars

A number of spacecraft have landed on Mars in the hope of finding evidence of life. The Viking spacecraft carried out experiments on the Martian surface. These included testing for microbes that might be in the soil, but no firm evidence was found for any living organisms.

Another experiment suggested that there seemed to be something in the Martian soil that destroyed carbon compounds that were taken to Mars as part of the investigation. (Carbon compounds are the basis of life on Earth.) However, one theory was that it was the strong ultraviolet radiation from the Sun that destroyed the carbon compounds. On Earth, the ozone layer in the atmosphere protects us from this ultraviolet radiation, but there is no ozone layer on Mars.

The results of the experiments on Mars were disappointing, but we may have been looking in the wrong place for signs of life.

3 Working with a partner, choose one of the following topics to carry out research on the internet.
- Viking mission to Mars
- Schiaparelli and the canals of Mars
- Demos and Phobos (moons of Mars)
- retrograde motion of the planets

Record the two best web addresses you find.

4 With a partner, view this website:

www http://core.nasa.gov/olr.html

Then prepare a short PowerPoint presentation on your findings.

The methane mystery

The gas used in Bunsen burners is called methane. It is a hydrocarbon made of just two elements, hydrogen and carbon. In 2004, evidence of methane was found in the thin Martian atmosphere. The gas was detected near icy patches on the surface. On Earth, virtually all the methane is produced from living things, so finding methane on Mars suggested that life might have once existed there. However, there is some evidence that on Earth methane can also be formed from reactions in rocks at high temperatures, so the same could have happened on Mars.

Travelling to Mars

There are many forces involved in a journey to Mars from the Earth. In order to begin the trip at all, the launch rocket must overcome the strong attraction of gravity. Once in space, the rocket will be affected by the gravitational pull of everything around it: other planets and especially the Sun.

If you have tried throwing a ball at someone who is running across your line of sight, the ball and the person must arrive together at the same place, or you will miss. With a game, this does not matter. With a spacecraft, if you miss the planet, you will have wasted a lot of effort and money. Scientists calculate the required speed and the total mass of the spacecraft so that, months or years later, the spacecraft and Mars arrive in exactly the same position.

To reduce the amount of fuel needed on the journey, spacecraft use 'planetary swing-by'. This means using the gravitational attraction of one planet to swing the spacecraft round towards another one. Calculations have shown that explorers could travel to Mars by starting off in the opposite direction. The spacecraft could be launched towards Venus, a planet closer than us to the Sun, and the gravitational attraction of Venus could be used to provide the energy needed for the spacecraft to reach Mars. The table shows possibilities for space journeys.

Destination	Total travel time	Possible launch frequency
Moon	7 days	many possibilities
Mars	2 years	every 2 years
Phobos	2 years	every 2 years

The planet Mars is smaller than Earth: its diameter is about half that of the Earth. The force of gravity of a planet is related to its mass. This means that your weight on Mars would be quite different from that on Earth.

5 Write your own answers to the questions below.

a If you were launched to Mars on your next birthday and stayed there for 6 months, how old would you be on your return to Earth?

b Would it be easier or harder for a rocket to take off from Mars than from Earth? Explain your answer.

c How would your mass compare on Mars and on Earth?

Olympus Mons

The largest known volcano in the Solar System is on Mars and is called Olympus Mons. At its base its diameter is 600 kilometres, and it is three times the height of Mount Everest.

In addition to volcanic craters, Mars has many impact craters. These were probably caused by collisions with asteroids. It has been estimated that an asteroid of 30 metres diameter would give a crater 1 kilometre across. All volcanoes on Mars are extinct, and one way to estimate the time since a Martian volcano was active is to count the number of impact craters in the volcano's crater: the older the volcano, the more craters. On this basis, Olympus Mons is the youngest volcano on Mars, and was active about 100 million years ago.

Review

Work in groups. Each group will be given a piece of A3 paper.

- Fold the paper into 4 quarters.
- As a group, think of four questions about Mars.
- Write down your questions, one on each quarter of the paper. Pass the paper to the next group.
- Answer the questions you have received, and prepare to discuss your answers with the whole class.

Chapter summary

In this chapter you have found out that:

- Mars and its moons have connections with myths.
- The elliptical orbit of Mars makes its size and brightness appear to change.
- There is no clear evidence of life on Mars.
- Spacecraft to Mars make use of the gravitational pull of other planets and the Sun.
- The largest known volcano in the Solar System is on Mars.

Friction

Introduction

In this chapter we look at friction and how it can be reduced or increased.

- Friction wears things down and produces heat.
- Friction can be useful or unhelpful.
- Friction increases with surface roughness.
- We can reduce friction by using lubricants.

If friction suddenly vanished, how would you get around without slipping over?

Friction facts

When you push your hand along a wooden table, a force acts against you. This is the force of friction. Friction always works against an object that is moving. Friction is an unusual force. It cannot start an object moving; it simply makes it harder for an object to start moving or slows it down.

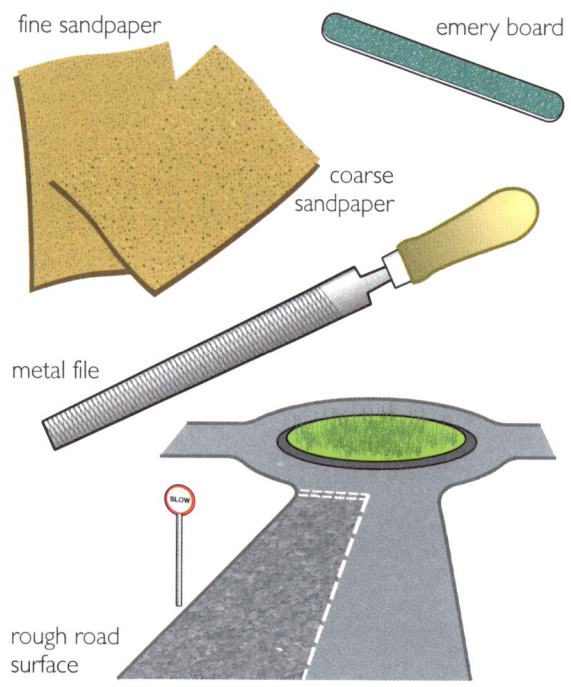

fine sandpaper

emery board

coarse sandpaper

metal file

rough road surface

These objects are designed to apply frictional forces.

1 You are going to generate heat by using frictional forces.

You will need:
- sandpaper strip
- rough wooden block
- thermometer

This is what you do:

1 Note the temperature of the room

2 Rub the sandpaper on the wood 50 times backwards and forwards

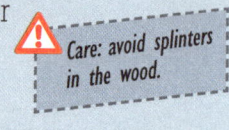

Care: avoid splinters in the wood.

3 Immediately wrap the sandpaper around the thermometer bulb and note any change

4 Repeat, rubbing 100 times

- Predict any changes this time

- What happens to the energy used to move the sandpaper against the rough wood surface?

A drill has to be harder than the material it drills into. The friction necessary to drill through rock requires the hardest natural material known – diamond. Diamonds are embedded in the surface of this drill bit.

How smooth is smooth?

Some surfaces look very smooth, such as a granite worktop in a kitchen, or a polished wooden table. If you look more closely, things seem rather different. Using a magnifying glass or a microscope, even the smoothest surface is seen to be uneven.

Heavy mud

To find new oil deposits underground, geologists need to drill down through solid rock. The frictional heating between the drill and the rock can damage the drill. Rock drills are studded with diamonds, the hardest natural material known, and damage would be expensive to put right.

The solution is to circulate a special mixture down the drill hole and back up to the surface. It is called 'drilling mud' and is an artificial mixture of minerals. One of them is barium sulphate, once called 'heavy spar' since it is so dense. The drilling mud does several useful jobs. It cools down the diamond drill, stopping it from overheating. The mud also carries bits of rock back to the surface. When geologists study the rock fragments, they can see if it is likely to contain oil.

3 You are going to study the smoothness of surfaces.

You will need:
- magnifying glass or microscope
- wooden ruler, newspaper, glossy magazine paper, matchstick

This is what you do:

1 Examine each surface carefully in bright light

2 Put the surfaces in order of smoothness, starting with the smoothest

- How could you make the smoothest surface even smoother?

The advantage of being smooth

Smooth surfaces reduce friction. If you want to push a cupboard across a floor, the surface makes a big difference to the force needed. Pushing the cupboard across smooth wooden floorboards is easy. Trying the same thing over a thick pile carpet is much harder, since the friction is so much greater.

4 For 'the big push', you will need:
- elastic band
- wooden block with a hook attached
- ruler or newtonmeter
- large flat board
- variety of surfaces to place on the board, such as carpet, vinyl tile, greaseproof paper, plastic bag

This is what you do:

1 Decide how you will estimate the force needed to overcome friction, either by measuring the stretch of the elastic band or using a newtonmeter

2 Attach the elastic band to the hook on the block

3 Pull the block across the board at a steady speed and make your estimate of the force needed

4 In turn, place each surface on the board and repeat the above

5 Draw a bar chart to display your results

- Which surface caused the most friction, and which the least?

Do speed skaters want friction to be high or low?

One way to avoid wasting energy

When cars have to brake to slow down, a lot of energy is wasted.

The chemical energy of the petrol fuel does several useful things. It moves the car and produces electricity for the lights and the sound system. When the driver brakes, the energy of motion of the car is turned into frictional heating in the brakes, plus a little sound if the brakes squeal.

Engineers have found a way to avoid this waste of energy. As the brakes are applied, the car's energy of motion is used to operate an electricity generator. The extra electricity is fed back to the battery.

The car can have two kinds of engine, a petrol engine and an electric motor. In towns, the driver then switches to use the electric motor driven by the battery and so reduces air pollution as well as saving energy.

5 Working with a partner, choose one of the following headings to carry out research on the internet into the effects of friction.
  ● space shuttle protective tiles
  ● friction matches
  ● regenerative braking in cars

Sports and friction

Sports shoes have special soles to give a good grip: they increase the friction between the shoe and the ground. Squash and basketball players need a good grip to allow them to change direction quickly without sliding.

The opposite is needed for ice yachts and toboggans that race across frozen ground. These need smooth runners to reduce the force of friction. The blades are narrow to reduce the area of contact with the icy ground.

If you want to ski all year round, the answer is to use a dry ski slope. The slope is made of plastic bristles, designed to reduce the force of friction acting on the skis. But if you fall, you can suffer a friction burn. As your hands skid across the ski slope, energy of motion is turned into frictional heating.

The lubricant advantage

Much of the time, we want to reduce the effects of friction. If it is not possible to make surfaces as smooth as we would like, the answer may be to use a lubricant. There is a special word for the study of how to decrease the effects of friction: it is called 'tribology'.

Lubrication is just one example. A thin film of a low friction material is spread between two surfaces to make it easier for them to move against each other. An example of a lubricant is the material of black pencil leads –

graphite. Many spinning parts of electric motors use graphite as a lubricant.

At home you must sometimes have found it difficult to open the lid of a jar. If the lid has traces of oil or fat on it, your hand may slip as you try to turn the lid. This is an unhelpful example of lubrication. You can increase the friction between the lid and your hand by wearing a rubber glove. This allows you to turn the top more easily.

Just rolling along

Another approach to reducing friction is to use rollers or ball bearings. When surfaces roll against each other there is less friction than when they slide.

It is easy to slide heavy luggage on to the rollers at airport customs.

There have been many theories about how people moved heavy objects before the invention of cranes. For example, how did people move the giant stones at Stonehenge or the blocks of stone used to build the pyramids? It is likely that early builders understood how to use rollers to reduce friction.

6 You are going to investigate the use of lubricants.

You will need:
- metal 10 g masses
- large wooden board and blocks
- black lead pencils, water and cooking oil

This is what you do:

1 Use some blocks to set up the board at an angle of about 30° to 40°

2 Release the 10 g mass from the top of the board to see how far it travels, and then adjust the slope until the mass travels to about half way down the board

3 Use the pencil to add a layer of graphite lubricant to the lower side of the 10 g mass. See if this makes a difference to how far it travels. Then clean off the graphite

4 Compare the effectiveness of graphite, water and oil put on the board itself

5 Rate the lubricants from best to worst.

7 Think about designing a low friction toy model, working with a partner to share ideas. As an example, you could think about a hovercraft where air is forced downwards and reduces friction, using a tin lid plus a balloon as the source of air. But try to think of an idea of your own.

- Write a description of how the toy works and include a drawing.

- Compare your idea with that of another group.

Favourable friction

Here are just some of the advantages of friction:

- Nails stay in wood because of friction between the metal and the wood fibres.

- Car tyres need a good grip on the road.

- Tree roots support a tree by friction with the soil. (After floods when the soil changes to mud, gales can easily blow trees over.)

- Parachutists rely on air resistance to slow them down.

- Seeds of some plants, such as dandelion, are designed to have enough air resistance to fall slowly. This means that the seeds spread out further.

Friction with the air ensures that dandelion seeds are widely dispersed.

Review

Divide the class into groups, each with a team captain. Discuss the questions, with the captain recording the answers.

- In sport, give examples of where we want to reduce friction.
- Are there any advantages to having friction?
- What is meant by frictional heating?
- How do lubricants work?

Chapter summary

In this chapter you have found out that:

- Friction occurs when two surfaces move against each other.
- Friction can produce heating effects, as in bicycle brakes.
- Friction is useful in car tyres, shoes and when opening jars.
- We try to reduce friction in sports such as skiing, ice skating and tobogganing.
- Lubricants between surfaces make them move more easily by reducing friction.

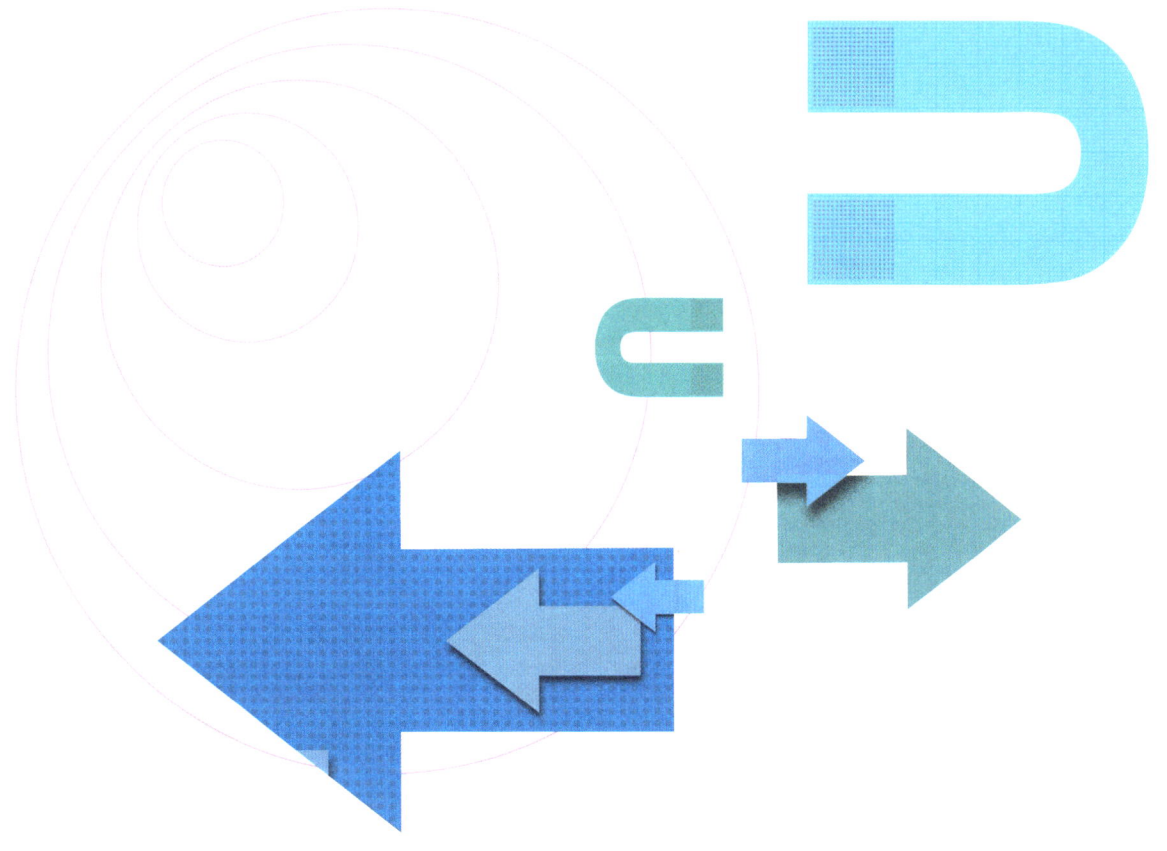

Streamlining

Introduction

In this chapter we look at how streamlining can reduce friction in air and water.

- Drag is the resistance to movement that anything experiences in air or water.
- Gases such as air, and liquids such as water, are all called fluids.
- Particles in air and water cause friction as an object moves through them.
- Streamlining can reduce drag.
- Living creatures have already solved the problem of streamlining.

Write down as many examples of streamlining in the natural world as you can think of.

Just a drag

If you want to cycle really fast downhill, it helps if you lean forward on the bike. You would go much slower if you were to sit upright and so form a larger barrier to the air you are moving through - you would have increased your air resistance, also called drag. Leaning down over the handlebars reduces drag, and the air can flow past you more easily.

At an Olympic velodrome, world-class cyclists add other ways to reduce drag and avoid wasting muscle power. They wear specially shaped helmets that allow air to flow past more smoothly. Their special clothing is close fitting for the same reason. The wheels of the bike are solid discs, since ordinary wheels with metal spokes create much more air resistance.

Indoor cycling demonstrates the art of streamlining.

Fast cars

Cars that were built a hundred years ago look very different from today's cars. Their top speeds were often less than 40 km per hour, and laws prevented them from going much faster. At such low speeds, air resistance was not a problem.

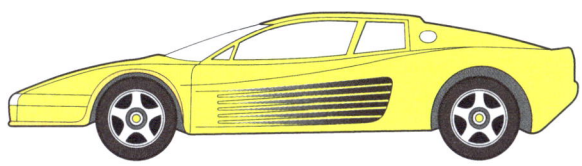

As speeds have increased, the design of cars has become more streamlined.

1 Using words, diagrams or both, describe two design changes in cars that have reduced air resistance.

2 You are going to have a model car race.

You will need:
- long, wide wooden slope
- 2 model cars (identical if possible)
- cardboard and tape
- fan or fan heater

This is what you do:

1 Cut two identical pieces of card to fix to the front of each model car

2 Fix one card to give a smooth curved surface over the car, front to back

3 Fix the other to act like a windscreen in an old car

4 Arrange the fan to blow air up the sloping surface

5 Release the cars from the top

6 Compare the effects of air resistance

7 Modify the card to give the least possible drag on one of the cars, and try again.

The designers of early locomotives did not see air resistance as a priority.

Modern train design minimises the effect of air resistance.

3 Work with a partner to answer these questions. When you have finished, compare your answers with another group.

a Why are modern trains the shape they are?

b How have modern trains reduced the drag of passenger coaches?

c Why do trains travel more slowly than planes?

Go for lift-off

When you watch birds fly it seems so easy. People have tried for thousands of years to copy the flight of birds. In Greek myth, Daedalus and his son Icarus thought they had solved the problem. They built wings out of wax and bird's feathers. The wings worked so well that Icarus made a fatal mistake. He flew too high, the Sun's heat melted the wax and he fell into the sea.

The first powered aircraft were designed partly on a trial-and-error basis: If it doesn't work, change it. It was not fully understood why a plane experienced lift – an upward force. Eventually designers realised that the lift force resulted from the shape of the wing surfaces. The upper, curved wing surface made air move more quickly over it and reduced air pressure above it. The difference in air pressure between the curved top and the flat lower surface was enough to lift the plane into the air.

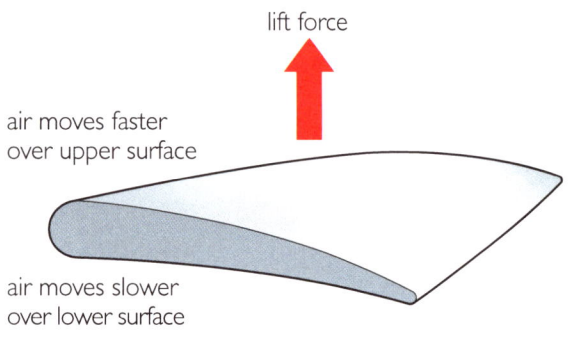

lift force

air moves faster
over upper surface

air moves slower
over lower surface

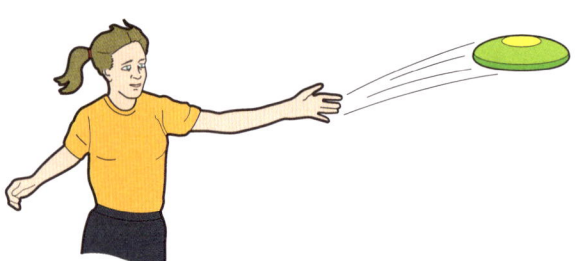

The curved, streamlined shape of the aircraft wing gives it lift when air flows over it. This shape is called an aerofoil; air flows over it easily and this reduces drag. Similarly, an upcurved shape helps keep a frisbee airborne.

4 You are going to test lift forces.

You will need:
- sheet of A4 paper
- hairdryer or your own lung power
- glue and thread

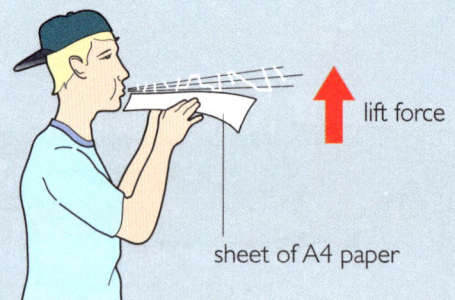

lift force

sheet of A4 paper

This is what you do:

1 Hold the sheet of paper by one edge below your mouth (see diagram), just touching the chin

2 Blow strongly and watch the lift force in action

3 Try the same idea using a hairdryer instead

support threads taped
to a wooden board

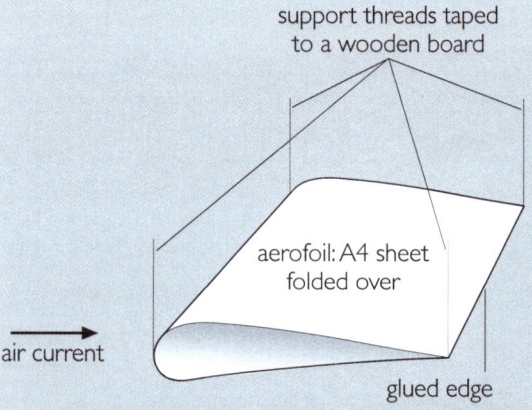

aerofoil: A4 sheet
folded over

air current

glued edge

4 Fold the sheet over itself and use glue to make a wing shape, curved on top, flat underneath

⚠ *Care: the glue gun gets very hot.*

5 Test this aerofoil using the hairdryer. It can be held in the right position using threads stuck on to a wooden board. The aerofoil rises when air is blown at it.

Ballooning

Since the eighteenth century, aeronauts have been designing and building balloons. The first balloons used hot air to provide lift. Later versions used hydrogen gas since it is much lighter than air and provides a strong lifting force. One disastrous idea was to combine the two, hydrogen and hot air. Hydrogen–air mixtures are explosive, as the unfortunate aeronauts demonstrated soon after take-off.

The major problem with ballooning is that you have no choice about where you are going. Balloons cannot be steered; they are simply carried along by the wind. The later development of airships solved this problem. Early airships had streamlined shapes and included a passenger cabin and engines. They also used hydrogen to provide the lifting force. After a series of explosions, a new lifting gas, helium, was chosen.

Streamlining helps airships navigate the skies.

Helium is still used. It is denser and more expensive than hydrogen but it is not flammable. Small helium airships are used for aerial photography and for advertising. Engineers have also designed large airships that could be used to move equipment in remote places that have no roads, for example to transport mobile phone masts. These ideas have yet to be tested to see if they work.

Drag in air and in water

If you want to race someone at the edge of the sea, there is an easy way to win. Make sure you run on the shore side in shallow water while your opponent has to run along in slightly deeper water. You experience drag as you run through the air but it is far less than through water. With deeper water to run through, your opponent has a much harder time: 'hydrodynamic' drag is much greater than the drag in air. Running through deeper water is very hard work.

Horses and lobsters

Racehorse owners sometimes train their horses in water tanks or in shallow water. As the horse swims, the extra drag of the water makes the horse work hard and build up muscle strength.

There have been reports from deep under the sea of lines of lobsters walking over the seabed like infants on a school trip. By attaching themselves to their neighbours, the lobsters form a more streamlined shape and so reduce the drag and speed up their migration.

5 You are going to test how streamlined different shapes are.

You will need:
- tall glass container of water
- plasticine or clay
- 2 elastic bands
- stopwatch

This is what you do:

1 Fix the elastic bands round the water container a known distance apart, say 30 cm

2 Roll the plasticine into a ball shape. Drop it into the water and time it as it falls between the two bands

3 Recover the plasticine and try different shapes such as cube, saucer or bullet shapes. Compare the times for each shape

4 Which shape has the least drag?

6 Working with a partner, choose one of the following topics to carry out research on the internet.

- streamlining in cars
- air resistance and cycling
- parachutes used as air brakes
- R101 airship

Submarine world

Early submarines were built of wood and were only designed for use in shallow water, such as a river. The air supply came from a simple hand-pump and a long tube that reached the surface. Modern submarines are rather different.

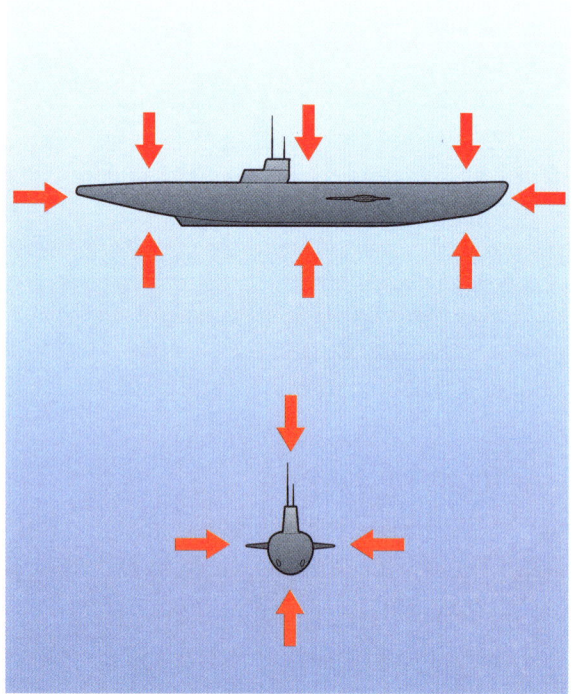

A submarine has a streamlined shape. It experiences pressure from all directions.

The near-circular cross-section of a submarine provides the strength needed to withstand the great pressures under the sea. When you dive down to the bottom of a swimming pool to find a coin, you can feel the pressure on your chest. Deep under the sea, the pressures are enormous.

The streamlined shape of a submarine reduces drag as it moves through the water. This reduces fuel consumption and causes less turbulence (stirring movement) in the water, helping the submarine to escape detection.

Natural streamlining

Sea creatures have evolved ways to reduce friction as they move through the water. Their streamlined shapes are ideally suited to reducing drag. Sharks are an example. They have a flexible skeleton made of cartilage, a type of protein. They have powerful muscles and a streamlined shape that allows them to move very fast.

Serious swimmers know a lot about the importance of streamlining. If your hair floats behind you as you swim, it increases drag and slows you down. If a swimmer's head is above water, it also increases drag. It creates waves at the surface and prevents the swimmer adopting the most streamlined shape to move through the water. To further improve their streamlining, swimmers wear close-fitting hats, body suits and goggles. All of these increase speed in the water.

Useful water friction

There are times when we want to increase friction with water. When you row a boat, if there were no friction between the oar blade and the water, the boat would not move. Boats with paddle wheels also rely upon friction with water to propel the boat along.

Review

Draw diagrams to explain the answers to each of the following questions. Do not use any words. Ask a partner to match each question with the correct diagram.

- What do we mean by drag?
- How do cyclists and swimmers reduce drag?
- Describe two examples of streamlining in the sea, one natural and one artificial.
- How do car designers reduce air resistance?

Chapter summary

In this chapter you have found out that:

- The frictional force resisting movement in gases and liquids is called drag.
- Streamlining is a way of reducing drag by changing the shape of objects, and sometimes the nature of their surfaces as well.
- Streamlining is important in designing cars, trains and aircraft since it reduces the waste of power.
- Sharks and other fish are natural examples of successful streamlining.

Magnetic attraction

Introduction

In this chapter we look at magnetic and non-magnetic materials and how we can make magnets.

- Magnets attract magnetic materials.
- Magnets have both north and south magnetic poles.
- Opposite magnetic poles attract, but two poles that are the same will repel.
- Magnetic materials can be turned into magnets.
- We use magnets in many different ways.

Think of some ways to use magnets. Discuss them with a partner.

Magnetic history

Some natural minerals are magnetic. The best known is called magnetite, an iron oxide. Ancient Greek myths refer to a mountain that can pull iron nails out of ships! One story tells of a shepherd whose iron-tipped crook stuck so strongly to a boulder that he could not pull it free again. Allowing for some exaggeration, it is clear that people recognised the attraction between magnets and iron a very long time ago.

The first person to describe the behaviour of magnets in detail was William Gilbert (1544–1603). He worked as a physician to Queen Elizabeth the First. (See more about Gilbert's ideas in Key Ideas: *Energy*, pages 74 and 75.) It was Gilbert who first said that the Earth itself was a giant magnet.

People already knew that a piece of magnetite, then called lodestone, could be used to find the direction of north. When a small piece of lodestone was tied to a thread and left to move freely, it always turned to point north. We now know the magnetic north pole and the geographical North Pole (the point on which the Earth spins) are in slightly different places, as you will see on page 47.

Pole position

When we investigate an ordinary bar magnet we find that the magnetism acts at its strongest at the ends. The ends are called north and south poles. If you break a magnet in half, the old poles stay the same and two new poles appear, one at each broken end.

1 Draw a long bar magnet and mark north and south poles. Draw a cut on the magnet and mark the new poles.

2 You are going to use a magnet to make another magnet.

You will need:

- bar magnet
- plotting compass
- thin iron or steel rod, e.g. a straightened paper clip
- metal cutters

This is what you do:

1 Bring the bar magnet near the compass, move it about and observe the changes

2 Stroke one end of the bar magnet all the way along the metal rod. Repeat 20 times, always in the same direction

3 Test the metal rod with the compass to see if it is now a magnet

4 Carefully cut the rod in half and test each half using the compass.

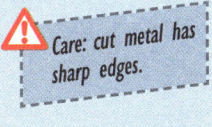

Care: cut metal has sharp edges.

You cannot have a single magnetic pole; poles always come in pairs, north and south. The magnetism is strongest at the poles.

Magnetic pole laws

When you bring two magnets together, you find that the magnetic poles behave differently. Opposite poles, north and south, attract each other:

Unlike poles attract.

If you bring two norths or two souths together, they repel each other:

Like poles repel.

These are the rules of magnetism.

3 Magnets attract magnetic materials, but magnets have no effect on non-magnetic materials.

To test for magnetic materials you will need:

- bar magnet
- selection of materials to test, including: glass, plastic, iron, copper, nickel spatula, wood, aluminium (can)

This is what you do:

1 Predict what will happen with each material

2 Bring each material separately to the bar magnet and find which are attracted

3 Make a list of magnetic and non-magnetic materials

Copper is an expensive metal, so modern coins often contain another metal inside, covered in a thin layer of copper.

4 Take a copper coin, such as a 2p piece, and test with the magnet

- Is it just copper, or is there evidence of another metal as well?

There are only three elements that show permanent magnetism. These are the metals iron, nickel and cobalt. Bar magnets are made of mixtures of these metals called alloys. Steel is also magnetic, since it is mostly made of iron. Magnetite (iron oxide) and ferromagnetic compounds called ferrites (containing iron, oxygen and other metals) can also be made into permanent magnets.

Magnetism is able to pass through some materials. If you wear magnetic earrings, the magnetism must cross the ear lobe or they would fall off. With a magnetic football game, the magnetism has to pass through the board so that you can make the players move round the field. There are some materials that don't let magnetism pass through them. One example is iron, a magnetic material!

4 Work with a partner to answer these questions. When you finish, explain your answers to another group.

a Which of these three metals can be described as magnetic – copper, iron, aluminium?

b How could you separate iron filings from sand?

c How would you use a magnet to separate steel food cans from aluminium drinks cans as they go past on a conveyor belt? Write down exactly what will happen to each type of can.

Flexible magnets

You can make magnets that bend from magnetic materials called ferrites – compounds containing iron. Ferrites are rigid (ceramic) materials but they can be ground to powder, then mixed with a plastic and moulded into shapes that are flexible. As magnets, they are reasonably strong, though not as powerful as a bar magnet. Fridge magnets have a piece of this material at the back which sticks to the steel of the fridge.

5 Does magnetism pass through paint?

6 To test which materials magnetism passes through you will need:
- bar magnet
- clamp stand
- thread and steel paper clip
- sticky tape
- selection of materials as for activity 3

This is what you do:

1 Fix the bar magnet to the stand

2 Tie the thread to the clip and arrange it vertically as in the diagram

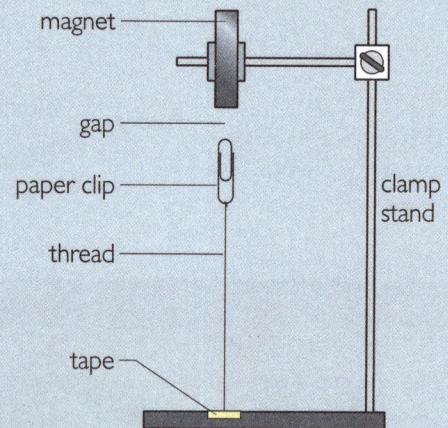

3 Place materials in the gap between the magnet and the clip

4 Make a note of your observations. Remember: Magnetism passes through non–magnetic materials

5 Name two magnetic and two non-magnetic materials.

Levitation by magnets

When trains travel over steel rails, a lot of energy is wasted overcoming the friction. There is friction in the wheel bearings on the axle and also between the wheels and the rails. If the train could float – levitate – above the track, there would be no friction. Magnets enable this to happen, and the trains, used widely in Japan, are known as as maglev trains. They have no wheels.

There are two sets of magnets, one set on the train and another in the track underneath. Since like poles are placed together, the train is repelled and floats just about the track. Maglev trains are very fast, but the special track is expensive to build and maintain.

7 **a** Why do maglev trains use like magnetic poles?

  b What would happen if they used opposite poles?

8 Working with a partner, choose one of the following topics to carry out research on the internet.

- maglev trains
- William Gilbert's theory
- lodestone (also spelt loadstone)
- ceramic magnets

Magnetic toys

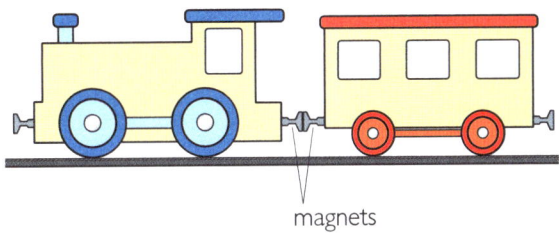

magnets

Wooden trains with magnetic couplings are ideal for young children since they are easy to join, attaching automatically, and easy to take apart. Iron filings, which are magnetic, are used in pictures which children can play with: the picture and loose filings are both under a plastic bubble, and when a magnet is moved under the picture, the filings form strange beards and hairstyles. In a third toy, magnetic football players are moved easily by moving a magnet under the board.

9 How could you make a magnetic train that would never join up?

10 Working with a partner, design a new kind of magnetic toy. Either sketch your design or describe how it works. Compare your idea with another group.

Medical magnets

When your work involves cutting metals, you must protect your eyes. Pieces of metal in the eye can cause severe damage to sight. The commonest metals we use contain iron and so are magnetic.

When an accident does happen, an eye surgeon can make use of the properties of magnets to help the patient. By placing a sharp pointed magnet near the piece of metal in the eye, it may be possible to remove it. The best kind of magnet to use is one that can be controlled by a switch so that it can be turned on and off (see page 54).

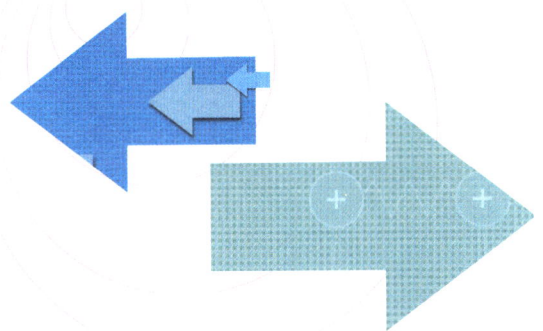

Magnetic rocks

Iron is quite common in the rocks of the Earth's crust. Iron minerals give the yellow and brown colours to most sands and sandstone. Molten lava from a volcano is likely to contain traces of iron. As the hot molten rock cools down, the iron particles act like small compasses. They point in the direction of the magnetic north pole at the time the rock solidified. By looking at the direction of these tiny magnets, geologists can use this natural magnetism in rocks to investigate how the rock has moved over millions of years. Whole continents move around very slowly, rather like gigantic icebergs in the sea. The study of these rocks is known as palaeomagnetism.

The test of a permanent magnet

When magnets are placed near each other, opposite poles attract and like poles repel each other. If a material is magnetic but is not a permanent magnet, either end will be attracted to a magnet. It follows, therefore, that the test for a magnet is that it must both attract and repel another magnet.

Review

Arrange for the statements below to be read out in turn. Use cards marked True and False to indicate your judgement on the statements.
- The magnetic north pole is not at the North Pole.
- Like poles attract.
- Copper is attracted by a magnet.
- Magnetism passes through non-magnetic materials.

Chapter summary

In this chapter you have found out that:
- Magnetism has been studied since ancient times.
- A magnet can be used to make another magnet by the method of stroking.
- Like magnetic poles repel and unlike poles attract.
- Permanent magnets are usually made from iron, cobalt or nickel, or alloys of these metals.
- Magnetism passes through non-magnetic materials such as paint or paper, but is stopped by magnetic materials such as iron.

Magnetic fields

Introduction

In this chapter we look at the magnetic field that surrounds a magnet.

- The Earth has a magnetic field.
- Magnetic field lines can be shown using iron filings or a plotting compass.
- The strength of a magnetic field gets less as you move further away from the magnet.
- The poles of a magnet can be called north-seeking and south-seeking.
- Magnetic fields can damage electronic equipment, including satellites.

Some birds can sense magnetic forces on Earth. Why might this be useful to them?

Finding out about our inner planet

The Earth is made of layers of different materials. In the centre is a solid core about the size of the Moon and made of iron and nickel. Round this is the outer core in which the iron and nickel are fluid. These metals are magnetic and can conduct electricity.

Scientists have different theories to explain why the Earth behaves like a giant magnet

with a magnetic field. One theory says that it is because the material in the outer core is circulating and, being a moving substance that can conduct electricity, it generates a magnetic field (we shall look at this in detail later). This system inside the Earth is known as the 'geodynamo'.

William Gilbert's idea

As we saw in the last chapter, the Elizabethan scientist William Gilbert first wrote about the magnetism of the Earth. That was in 1600. The following extract from a science book published in 1840, a few years after Queen Victoria was crowned, comments on Gilbert's observations.

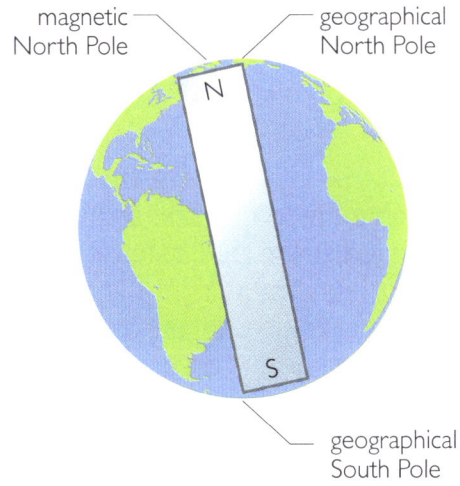

The Earth is a spherical magnet.

Gilbert had then observed that small bars of an iron window frame, placed north and south, which had remained many years in the same position, were become magnetic. He observed also that if a bar of iron, placed north and south, be brought to red heat in a forge, and be then beat on the anvil in the same position, it will acquire the magnetic virtue. Gilbert says that if a spherical form be given to a magnet, and if its two poles be at the extremities of a diameter, this spherical magnet when suspended on its poles, will turn round its axis in twenty four hours. For as the Earth, adds he, is but a large magnet, it must have a similar motion.

The French scientist Petit made the experiment proposed by Gilbert and the small magnetic globe remained perfectly motionless. Another philosopher concluded, from the failure of Gilbert's experiment, that the Earth was motionless.

1 Work with a partner. When you finish, explain your answers to another group.

a Which important direction does Gilbert note in his observations?

b What happened to the ordinary iron bars of the window frame?

c Is the evidence from Gilbert's experiment enough to prove that the Earth does not rotate once every 24 hours? Explain your reasoning.

What is a magnetic field?

The region around a magnet, where it has a magnetic effect, is called the magnetic field. The Earth's magnetic field extends millions of kilometres into space. The magnetic field of a bar magnet is much smaller and is easy to find.

2 You are going to plot a magnetic field.

You will need:
- bar magnet
- large piece of card
- iron filings
- plotting compass
- safety goggles

 Wear safety goggles.

This is what you do:

1 Place the magnet under the card, in the centre

2 Sprinkle iron filings over the card, then tap it gently

3 Observe the pattern of the magnetic field lines. Carefully remove the iron filings

4 Repeat step 1. Move the compass right around the magnet, each time drawing a small arrow for the direction it points in

5 Observe the pattern.

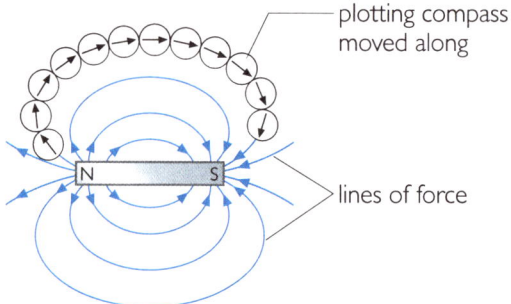

The magnetic field of a bar magnet.

The lines you see formed by the filings show the shape of the magnetic field around a bar magnet. We call them 'lines of force'. The compass shows us two things. It shows the shape of the magnetic field and also the direction of the magnetic force. We say that the lines of force run from the north pole of the magnet to its south pole. On drawings, we add arrows on the lines of force, pointing from north to south.

3 Look carefully at the diagram, then draw it from memory, including the arrows. Check your answer with the original drawing.

Magnetism at a distance

A compass needle is a magnet. With a compass at a pole of a bar magnet, the compass needle points in a straight line either towards or away from the pole. As you move the compass further away from the bar magnet, the magnetic field becomes weaker. Eventually, the field of the magnet is so weak that the compass points in its normal direction, that is, towards the Earth's north magnetic pole. Since opposite poles attract, we can work out which of the Earth's *magnetic* poles is at the *geographical* North Pole.

4 The north-seeking end of a compass needle points towards the geographical North Pole. Is this end of the compass a magnetic north pole or a magnetic south pole?

Magnetism is in 3D

The magnetic field around the Earth stretches out into space in all directions: it is three-dimensional. The field around a bar magnet is also 3D, even though we usually see it flat using iron filings.

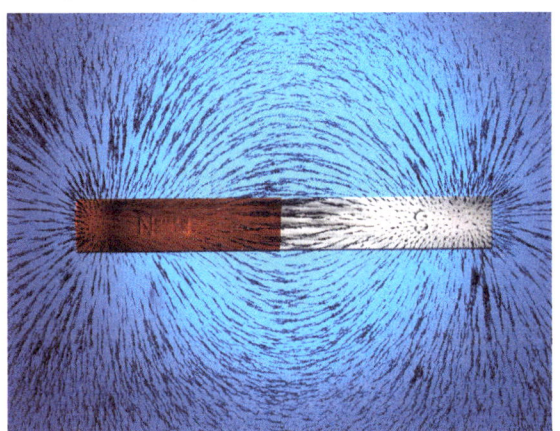

Magnetic fields are three-dimensional.

5 Work in pairs for this magnetic map puzzle.

You will need:
- bar magnet and plotting compass
- large card and books for support
- grid of large-squared graph paper

This is what you do:

1 Rest the grid and card on the supporting books

2 Hide the magnet underneath

3 Ask your partner to choose 10 squares on which you will place the compass

4 Your partner then uses observations of the compass needle at these positions to locate the hidden magnetic poles

- Can you use a sheet of iron or aluminium in place of the card for this puzzle? Explain your answer.

Finding your way around

In ancient times, sailors had no maps and used to rely on the positions of the stars to help them navigate. It was much later that people began to use the Earth's magnetic field to help them. Unfortunately, the Earth's geographic North Pole (the spin axis) is not in the same place as the magnetic north pole. To add to this, the magnetic pole moves a little each year. Consequently, navigators use up-to-date correction tables to adjust for the differences in direction of the two poles.

Nowadays, ships are often fitted with GPS, the global positioning system. This is a satellite navigation system based on the time taken for a signal to travel from more than one satellite to the ship. But in case there are difficulties in satellite communication, navigators still need to rely on the Earth's magnetism.

Lodestone history

It was the Chinese who discovered how to make the first compass. They knew about the natural magnetic properties of the iron mineral magnetite (lodestone) which you read about in the last chapter.

Some 2000 years ago, Chinese fortune tellers used a magical spoon to tell the future. It was called the 'south-pointing spoon' and was made from lodestone. Later versions used a magnetic iron needle that could be used for navigation. The needles were magnetised by two different methods. In one, the iron was stroked with a piece of lodestone to turn it into a magnet. In the other method, the iron was made red hot in a fire and laid to cool in a north-south direction. The effect of the Earth's field made the iron into a magnet. These were the same methods used by William Gilbert hundreds of years later. According to Gilbert, every magnet has 'an invisible orb of virtue' around it that affects iron.

Birds may use the Earth's magnetic field when they migrate.

Animal magnetism

Some creatures seem to be able to use the Earth's magnetic field to navigate as they migrate across the world. There are several possible explanations for this ability.

Sharks seem to be able to sense the magnetic field as small electric currents in their bodies: these currents are produced as the shark swims through the lines of magnetic force. Another theory is based on crystals of magnetite that have been found in the brains of some animals, including humans. It is not yet understood how these magnetic crystals help creatures find an exact position on Earth.

6 With a partner, choose one of the topics to research on the internet.
- Earth's magnetic field
- bird migration
- magnetic reversal
- history of the compass

Prepare a short PowerPoint presentation on your topic.

7 You are going to demonstrate a magnetic field in 3D.

You will need:
- plastic tube, closed at one end
- bar magnet that fits in the tube
- jar of a clear liquid such as syrup
- iron filings

This is what you do:

1 Mix some iron filings thoroughly with the syrup in a jar

2 Fix the empty tube upright in the mixture

3 Lower the magnet into the tube and watch

4 Observe how the filings move slowly in the thick liquid to show the shape of the magnetic field.

Magnetic destruction

Bank cheques and postage stamps have information printed on them using magnetic ink. Machines are able to read this information instantly. Magnetic storage of information has been widely used (although newer technologies are replacing magnetic storage). Old music cassettes and VHS cassettes use magnetic tapes to store sound and pictures. Some credit cards have a magnetic strip that carries important information. All of these magnetic storage devices can be damaged or made useless by strong magnetic fields. The field can rearrange the magnetic particles and so destroy the useful information.

The surface of the Sun is a violent place. At regular intervals, sunspots appear on the disc of the star. These dark areas are linked to intense magnetic fields within the Sun.

One effect of the magnetic fields is that streams of high-energy particles radiate from the Sun and destroy electronic equipment on Earth satellites. So, a magnetic storm 150 million kilometres away can make your satellite TV screen go blank or cut off your long-distance phone call.

Review

Divide the class into teams, each with a team captain. Each team discusses the questions and the captain records the answers.

- How would life be different if the Earth's magnetic field disappeared overnight?
- How can you show that a magnetic field gets weaker as you move away from a magnet?
- Describe two uses of magnetite (lodestone).
- What kinds of things can be damaged by strong magnetic fields?

Chapter summary

In this chapter you have found out that:

- The Earth has a magnetic field that extends in three dimensions in space.
- Lines of magnetic force can be shown using iron filings or a compass.
- The strength of a magnetic field increases as you get closer to the magnet.
- Magnetic fields can destroy or damage information stored using magnetic ink or tape.

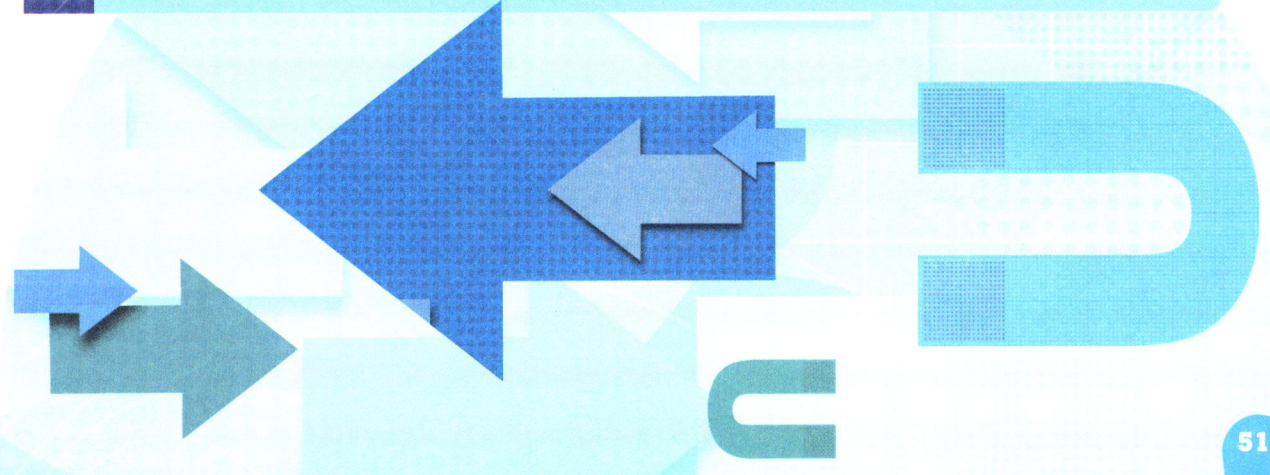

Electromagnets

First clues

Lightning is an electrical discharge between storm clouds and the ground. It has been known for a long time that bolts of lightning can make iron magnetic, and so people decided that there must be a link between electricity and magnetism.

The proof came in 1819 when the Danish professor Hans Oersted made an important observation. He wanted to show the heating effect of an electrical current flowing in a straight wire. There was a compass near the wire. When he switched the current on, the compass needle moved to a new direction. When he switched off again, the needle went back to normal. He extended the experiment by seeing what happened to metal filings when the current was on. As with a bar magnet, he found that iron filings formed a pattern, but copper filings were not affected at all.

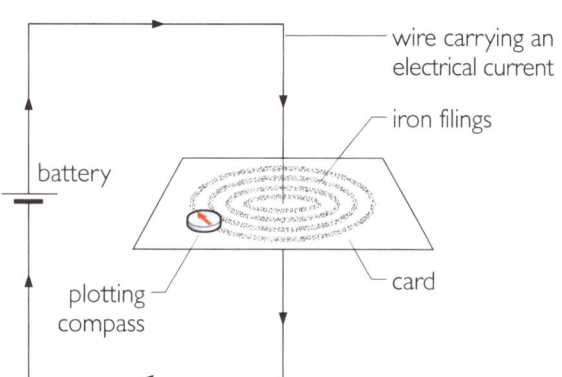

Oersted proved that there is a magnetic field when a current of electricity flows in a wire.

1 You are going to repeat Oersted's experiment.

You will need:
- low voltage supply, 4–6 V battery
- insulated wire about 2 m long
- compass
- small cardboard tube

This is what you do:

1 Connect the straight wire to the power supply

2 Place the compass near the wire. Then gradually move it away while observing the compass needle

3 Also observe any changes as the current is switched on or off

4 Replace the straight wire with a coil: use the cardboard tube to wind a coil of wire and repeat the experiment

5 Compare the strength of the magnetic field in straight and coiled wires by seeing how much the compass needle moves and how far away you can detect the magnetic field.

The first electromagnet

Not long after Oersted's experiment, the English scientist William Sturgeon developed a powerful magnet that could be switched on and off. He took a piece of iron and bent it into the shape of a horseshoe. A long insulated wire was coiled around the iron. When the current was switched on, the iron horseshoe became a very strong magnet.

The iron itself was not a permanent magnet but it increased the strength of the magnetic field round the wire. (The coil on its own produced a weaker field.) Sturgeon had therefore discovered the importance of putting an iron core inside an electrical coil or 'solenoid'. This arrangement, made up of a current-carrying wire coil round an iron bar, is called an 'electromagnet'.

2 Working with a partner, choose one of the following topics to carry out research on the internet.
- Oersted's experiment
- solenoids
- electromagnets in history
- Ampère's swimming man rule

The immense power of the electromagnet

The description below is taken from *Cyclopaedic Science Simplified* published in 1870.

1 ton = 20 hundredweight, written cwt, and equivalent to 1016 kg.
1 inch = 2.5 cm.
1 pound, written lb, is about 450 g.

When the immense power of the electro-magnet was ascertained, great anticipations were formed of the application of the force as a motive power. The great electromagnet made by Mr Apps will lift five hundred-weight using a single electrical cell. The Prince Consort [husband to Queen Victoria] asked if the electromagnetic power increased or decreased with the distance from the magnet. The following instructive figures explain this.

Lifting power	Distance from the electromagnet
36 lb	1/50 of an inch
47 lb	1/84 inch
90 lb	1/250 inch
220 lb	In contact with no gap at all

3 You are going to build an electromagnet and find out how to vary its strength.

You will need:
- several metres of insulated wire
- compass
- variable low voltage supply
- for the cores: large iron nail or iron bar; aluminium bar or copper rod
- steel paper clips
- 2 clamp stands

This is what you do:

1 Wind the wire into two separate coils, one with twice as many coils as the other. Place each coil round a core

2 Connect the power and use a compass to check that there is a magnetic field

Sc1 You can compare the strength of different electromagnets by seeing how many paper clips will hang from the core when the electromagnets are fixed vertically.

3 a Vary the number of turns of wire

   b Place an iron or aluminium or copper core in the coil

   c Vary the current by altering the voltage; use 3 V, then 6 V

• Stronger magnets will attract more steel paper clips. What is the best combination of turns of wire and type of metal core to give the strongest electromagnet?

Electromagnets used in scrapyards are strong enough to lift large iron and steel masses.

On-off magnetism

Bar magnets are magnetic all the time: they are permanent magnets. Electromagnets are only magnetic when the current flows through the wire coil. This on-off property is useful in everyday devices.

The current effect

Since the flow of an electrical current in a wire produces a magnetic field, changing the size of the current is likely to change the field strength. The best combination of properties to make a strong magnet is:

● increase the number of coils of wire

● use an iron core inside the coil

● increase the current

4 Why can electromagnets lift heavy cars but not light tyres?

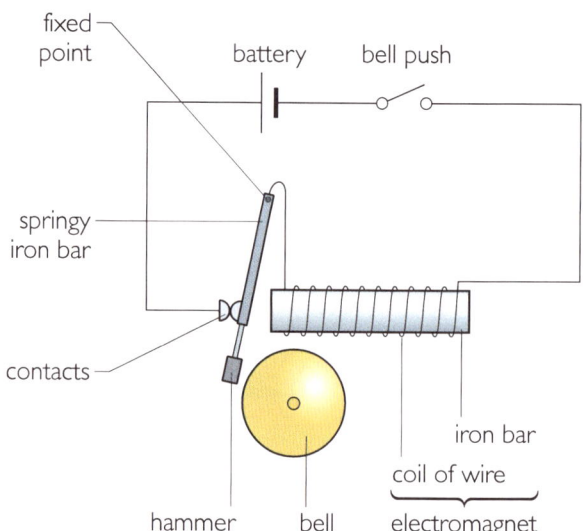

Using an electromagnet to ring the bell.

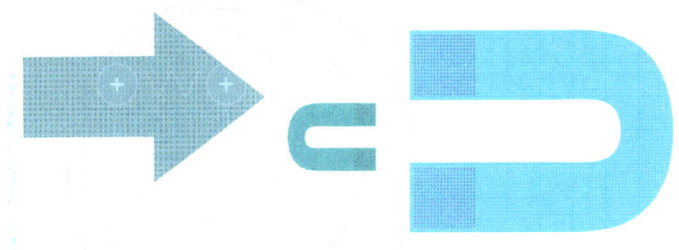

The bell circuit works like this.

● Press the bell push, the circuit is completed and electricity flows.

● The electromagnet is now on, and attracts the springy iron bar attached to the hammer.

● The hammer moves and hits the bell.

● When the iron bar moves towards the electromagnet, it breaks the circuit at the contacts and electricity stops flowing.

● With the electromagnet off, the spring takes the hammer back to the start position.

As long as the bell push is being pressed, this rapid cycle is repeated.

5 Think of three different uses for electric bells.

How can this be done without overheating the circuit? The answer is to break the circuit in two and use a special type of switch between circuits called a 'relay'.

The driver's key switches on a small current in the first circuit, which has long wires and an electromagnet at a relay switch. Turning the key closes this first circuit and the electromagnet generates a magnetic field. The field attracts the iron bar, the contacts close and the second, much shorter, circuit is completed. The high-power battery in the second circuit then gives a large current and this turns on the starter motor.

The relay circuit in a car.

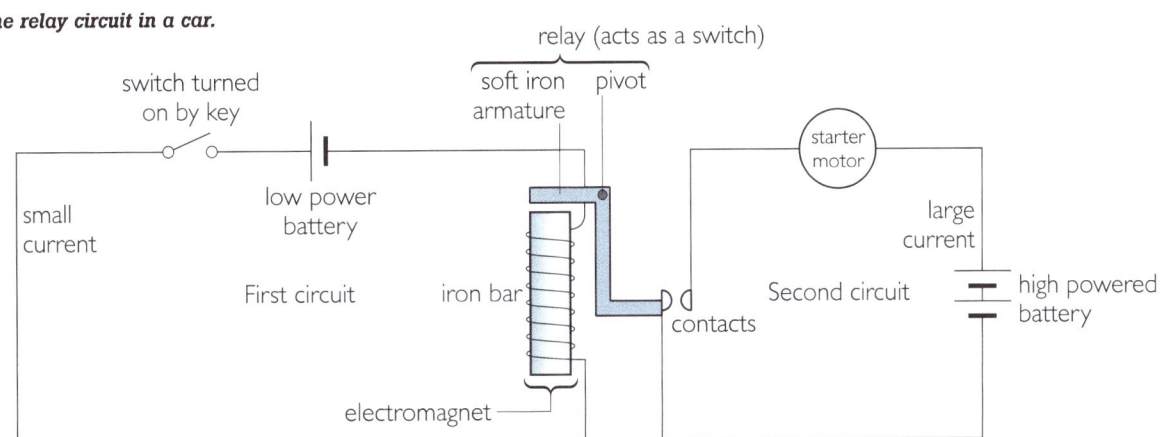

The current used to start a car engine is very big – about 100 amps. Compare this with the ordinary 3-pin plug at home that can take a maximum of 13 amps. The bigger the current, the shorter the connecting wires need to be, because, if the wires are long, the large current could heat them up and cause a fire.

To start a car, a driver wants to sit inside and just turn a key, not have to open the bonnet and engine compartment. This arrangement would need long wires linking the key to the high-power battery and starter motor.

6 a Why do we use short, thick connecting wires from a car battery to the starter motor?

b Lifts in shops use very large currents. What type of switch should be used? Explain your answer.

Electrical transport starts slowly

In the nineteenth century, the main source of power for factories and ships was the steam engine. When electromagnetism was discovered, inventors began to plan new kinds of engines.

One idea was based on the strong pull you get with a powerful electromagnet. It did not work very well. In 1837 Davidson placed an electromagnetic locomotive on the Edinburgh and Glasgow Railway. The carriage weighed about 5 tons but, when put in motion, a speed of only 4 miles per hour could be obtained.

Then Professor Jacobi of St Petersburg in Russia designed an electromagnetic boat engine. He tried it out on the River Neva. He found that it was powerful enough to propel twelve passengers at 3 miles an hour. It was many years before electric motors were developed that could provide a real alternative to steam engines.

7 Early electromagnets used electricity from batteries filled with strong acids. Why might this be dangerous?

Review

Write an answer to each question and exchange questions with a partner. Discuss any answers where you cannot agree.
- How can you make an electromagnet from a battery, some wire and a nail?
- Describe one difference and one similarity between bar magnets and electromagnets.
- Give one use of electromagnets.
- Give three ways to make an electromagnet stronger.
- Why do we use an electromagnetic switch in a car's starting system?

Chapter summary

In this chapter you have found out that:
- Electricity flowing in a wire produces a magnetic field.
- The field is stronger if the wire is coiled.
- The power of an electromagnet can be increased by using more coils, a higher current and adding an iron core.
- Electromagnets are used to lift heavy metal objects and to operate electric bells.
- A relay switch is an electromagnetic switch where a small current can switch on a much larger current, as in a car starting system.

On the turn

Introduction

In this chapter we look at turning forces and their uses:

- The turning effect of a force is called its moment.
- Things turn around a pivot.
- The turning effect of a lever depends on the force applied and its distance from the pivot.
- Tools, machines and people contain examples of levers.

 Think of different ways a screwdriver could be used as a lever.

Leverage

Most of the levers we use are made of metal because of its strength, and we use levers to transfer force. A lever is a bar that turns about a pivot. The force is applied to a point of resistance. Study the different lever arrangements in the diagram below.

In every case, there are three important things to notice about levers. The first is the force needed to make something happen. The second is the pivot. The last is the resistance: the object to which we are transferring the force is providing the resistance. For example, the metal top of a bottle resists the force that is being applied to the bottle opener.

Let us look at the position of the three points. The can opener has the force at one end, the resistance at the other end and the pivot in the middle. (Fulcrum is another name for a pivot.) We can arrange the three things in different orders. With a heavy wheelbarrow, the resistance is in the middle.

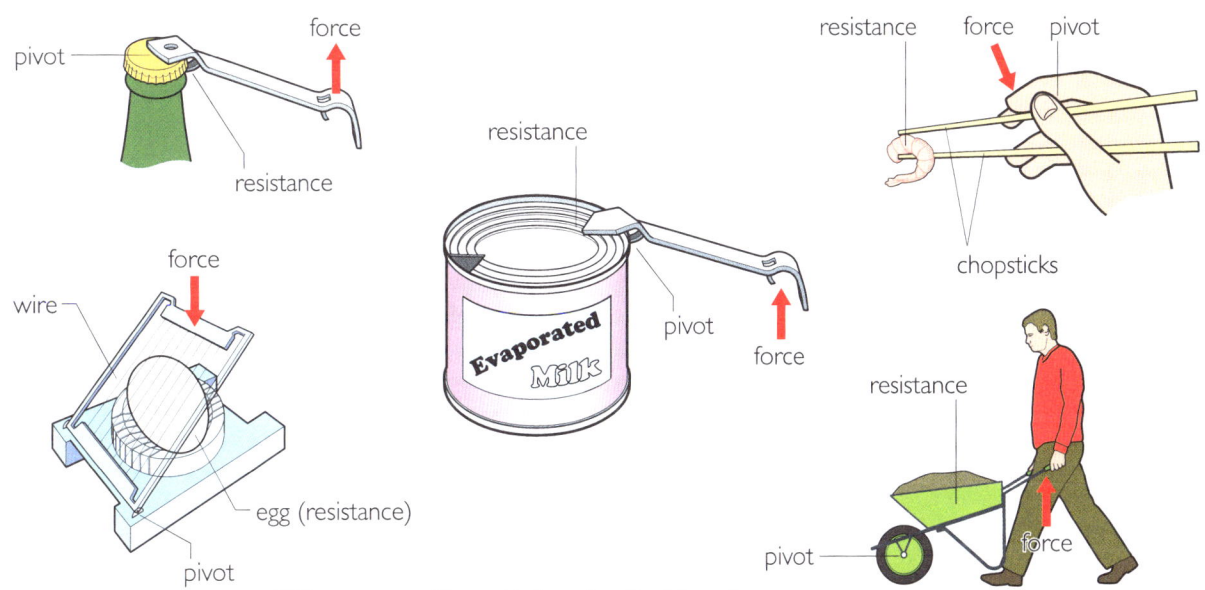

Different types of lever. Each makes the job easier.

1 You are going to use a lever to remove a nail.

You will need:

- strong length of wood for the lever
- screw-in eyelet
- wooden block
- nail and hammer
- clamp
- triangular piece of wood for the pivot
- bucket and string
- water or sand

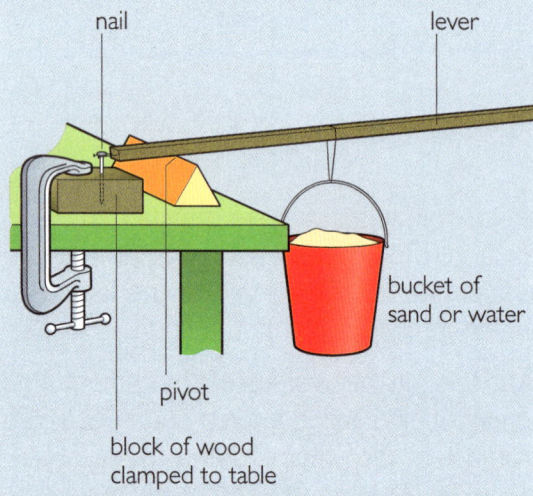

This is what you do:

1 Set up the apparatus as shown

2 Start with the bucket half way along the bar

3 Pour water or sand into the bucket until the nail begins to come out of the wood

⚠ *Care: do not let the heavy bucket fall on you.*

4 Investigate the effect of moving the bucket further away from the nail

- What is the connection between when the bucket falls and starts to remove the nail, and the distance between the bucket and the nail?

Force and distance rule

If you want to move a gigantic block of stone, the length of the lever you choose will make a big difference. Think about having a choice of two levers. One is the size of a big spoon, and the other is a metre long. In each case, you put the end of the lever under the stone and push down on the other end. Even as a thought experiment, it is clear which will be easier.

(a)

(b)
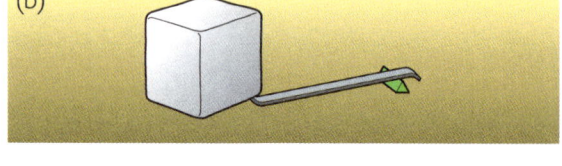

(c)
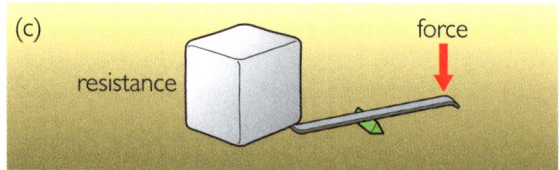

(d)

(e)

The force required to lift a block can be lessened in different ways.

By moving the pivot closer to the block, a smaller force can be used to raise the block, but by a smaller distance. By using a longer lever, even less force is needed to raise the block. Either way, it is much easier than using a short lever.

Archimedes and the Roman fleet

The Greek scientist and philosopher Archimedes lived in the port city of Syracuse whose walls were close to the sea. He designed weapons based on levers to repel an attack of the invading Roman fleet.

The Romans used long ladders from their fighting ships to enable soldiers to climb the walls. As soon as the ladders were in place against a wall, the Greeks swung levers out over them and dropped stones and lead blocks on to the soldiers below. After use, the beams were swung round on their pivots and could be reloaded with fresh stones.

Another device lowered an iron hook on to a ship below. Once the hook was caught fast on the ship, the lever was raised, pulling the front of the ship out of the water. The stern went down and the ship could be sunk. The defence of Syracuse using levers was a success on this occasion.

All in a moment

2 You are going to investigate the seesaw effect.

You will need:
- long piece of wood and pivot to make a model seesaw
- ruler
- several 10 g and 100 g masses (1 kg = 10 N)

This is what you do:

1 Balance the model seesaw without any masses

2 Place one mass right at one end. Add double this mass to the other side and balance it

3 Repeat for other combinations of masses

Each mass produces a downward force owing to the attraction of the Earth's gravity.

4 Each time, record the force of the mass at each end and the distance of each mass from the pivot

5 Compare your results with these sample results:

Force on left (N)	Distance to pivot (cm)	Force × distance
10	20	200

Force on right (N)	Distance to pivot (cm)	Weight × distance
20	10	200

 • What do you notice about the force × distance for each when they are in balance?

In activity 2, by multiplying weight by distance, you calculated the 'turning effect' of the force.

The turning effect of a force is called its moment.

The rule says:

Moment of a force = force (in newtons) × perpendicular distance (usually in metres) from the force to the pivot.

With small distances it is easier to use centimetres rather than metres. If the turning force is in the same direction as a clock moves, it is the clockwise moment. The opposite direction is the anti-clockwise moment. The Principle of Moments described first by Archimedes is that:

Total clockwise moment
= total anti-clockwise moment

– as when a seesaw is in balance.

This is why people of different weights must sit at different distances from the centre of a seesaw if they want to balance.

Weighing machines

You can make a weighing machine that uses the idea of moments. If you know the size of one weight and both distances, you can calculate the other weight.

4 To make a weighing machine, you will need:
- metre rule with a hole or pivot at the centre
- one known weight with a thread loop attached
- several unknown weights such as stones, each with loops attached

This is what you do:

1 Balance the metre rule with a central pivot

2 Place the known weight and one unknown weight on opposite sides of the pivot, and move them to balance

3 Note down the two distances and calculate the clockwise and anti-clockwise moments. Work out the unknown weight

Sc1 **4** Compare your results with results using a normal balance
- How accurate is the balance you have made?

5 Sketch and label a weighing machine that could be used to measure your own weight safely.

Human levers

When we lift weights at the gym, our arms can be seen as examples of levers. The equipment at the gym contains examples of levers as well. In a sport like rowing, the oar is the lever and the rowlock is the pivot.

5 Describe an example of a lever you find at the gym or playing a sport.

6 For this activity on tricks and balances, you will need:
- empty match box
- coins
- sticky tape
- large bottle cork
- two metal forks
- pin
- sharp pencil

This is what you do:

1 Open the matchbox and inside it tape the coins together at one end. Close the box

2 Place the box on a table edge. The hidden coins allow it to project from the edge without falling off

3 Stick a needle through the centre of the cork so that it shows through. Push the sharp ends of the forks into the cork on opposite sides The cork will now balance on the point of a pencil

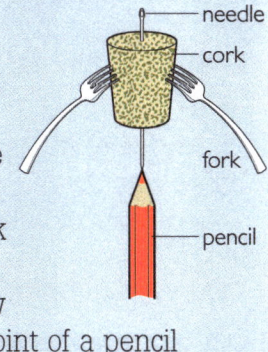
needle
cork
fork
pencil

4 Explain what you see in terms of the principle of moments.

Fairground rides

Some of the rides at the fairground use turning forces. As a ride spins round, you can often experience a change in the force of gravity. As the force increases, you can be pushed back into your seat and find it hard to raise your arms. Similarly, if you were on a bigger planet than the Earth, the greater gravitational attraction would make all your movements more difficult.

7 Where would it be better to go to break the distance record for hitting a golf ball, Earth or the Moon? Explain your answer.

8 Working with a partner, choose one of the following topics to carry out research on the internet.
- physics of toys
- science at the fairground
- weighing machines
- physics at the gym

Record the two best web addresses you find. Prepare an illustrated two-minute talk about your most interesting findings. You can use PowerPoint for your presentation.

Review

Divide the class into four teams, each with a team captain. Each team discusses the following topics with the captain recording the answers.
- Describe two examples of levers used at home.
- In arm wrestling, why does the person with longer arms have an advantage?
- Explain the principle of moments using a seesaw as an example.
- Give an example of a sport that uses levers.

Chapter summary

In this chapter you have found out that:
- A moment is the turning effect of a force.
- The force turns about a pivot or fulcrum.
- You calculate the moment by multiplying the force in newtons by the perpendicular distance to the pivot.
- When clockwise and anti-clockwise moments are equal, the forces either side of a pivot are balanced.
- There are levers in tools, in machines and in the body.

Under pressure

Introduction

In this chapter we look at how objects exert pressure and how this can be spread out or concentrated.

- The effect of a force depends on the area to which it is applied.
- Pressure is calculated by dividing the force by the area.
- Examples of concentrating force into a small area include nails and cutting edges.
- Examples of spreading a force over a large area include skis and the foundations of buildings.

Imagine the same person stepping on your hand, first wearing trainers and then in stiletto heels. Why is one more painful?

Force and area

The same size force can have different effects, depending on the area over which the force is acting. Think of pushing a drawing pin into wood; imagine trying point first and then flat head first. In one case, the pin goes into the wood. In the second case, it is impossible, using the same amount of force, to push the drawing pin into the wood.

The same mass can apply a different pressure, depending on the area.

We say that pressure is force per unit area:

$$\text{Pressure} = \frac{\text{force (in newtons)}}{\text{area (in square metres)}}$$

Think about this example.

A 1 litre bottle of water has a mass of 1 kg. On Earth, the force of gravity makes 1 kg weigh about 10 N. So the bottle weighs 10 N.

The two ends of the bottle have different areas.
The top has an area of 5 cm².

This is the same as $\frac{5}{10\,000}$ m²

The base of the bottle has an area of 50 cm².

This is the same as $\frac{50}{10\,000}$ m²

How do the pressures under the bottle of water compare, depending on which way up it stands?

Standing on its top:

$$\text{pressure} = \text{force/area}$$
$$= \frac{10}{(5 \div 10\,000)} = 20\,000 \text{ N/m}^2$$

Standing on the base:

$$\text{pressure} = \text{force/area}$$
$$= \frac{10}{(50 \div 10\,000)} = 2000 \text{ N/m}^2$$

The base has an area 10 times larger than the top, and applies a pressure 10 times less than the top. So, when the bottle is turned upright, the same force of 10 N has been spread out over an area that is 10 times larger.

High pressure ideas

Sometimes we want to increase pressure by reducing the area. Here are some examples.

Pressure is increased when force is applied over a very small surface area.

Nails have sharp points so that there is a high pressure on the wood when the nail is hit with a hammer. (The same idea is used with sharpened fence posts.) The sharp and blunt edges of a knife blade need different amounts of force to cut through cheese. Using the same force each time, the sharp edge gives a higher pressure since the area is smaller. It cuts more easily.

Ancient physics

The first people known to use technology based on the idea of pressure lived in the Stone Age. The material they chose for axes, knives and weapons was often flint – chemically the same compound as sand. Flint is a hard mineral and, when hit at an angle, it breaks to give a very sharp edge. Because the fracture is slightly curved, it is described as conchoidal, meaning 'like a shell'.

Stone Age people were experts at chipping flint into shapes that they used as axes to cut wood, arrowheads for hunting and knives to skin animals. When the edge became blunt, the pressure was reduced and the tools didn't cut very well. Fortunately, flint is a common material, so the tools were easy to replace.

Pressure on precious objects

When you buy gold or silver jewellery it is a good idea to look for the hallmark. Hallmarks have been used since 1300 to guarantee the quality of the metal. Once the jeweller has made the object, it is tested and then hallmarked at an assay office.

USA, 1715 – 1740

Edinburgh

Florence (Italy), 18th century

London

Stockholm (Sweden), 16th century

These hallmarks on silver show that the jewellery is good quality, and where, and often when, it was made.

Hallmarking uses the idea of pressure to mark valuable metals. The hallmark, different for each assay office, is a raised design on a small rod, which is made of a very hard metal. The design is held against the precious metal and the rod is struck with a hammer. The pressure is enough to mark the object.

1 Why does a heavy table leave deeper marks on a carpet than a wooden chest of the same weight?

Living over the water

Some of the earliest human settlements were lake villages where houses were built on stilts over the water. Some modern holiday homes use the same idea, especially around ports. The Romans used pointed stakes to support bridges over the River Thames. In Venice, the great palaces along the Grand Canal are built on a framework of pointed wooden stakes driven into the mud. In every case, the builders used the idea of concentrating the force into a small area – the point of the stake – to increase the pressure and drive the stake in more easily.

2 To 'stake out the pressure', you will need:
- bucket of sand or soil
- stick, sharp at one end, flat at the other
- ruler
- set of masses and hook or bag to attach to the stick

This is what you do:

1 Set the stick vertically in the sand and measure the length above the surface

2 Add masses until the stick begins to sink in. Continue until it has moved by 2 cm

Sc1 **3** Predict how much you need to add to make the stick move by another 2 cm

4 Repeat using the flat end of the stick in the sand

5 Compare the two sets of results and explain any differences.

Electric crystals

When you apply pressure to certain special kinds of crystal, they produce an electric charge. The charge is positive on one side of the crystal and negative on the other, an effect first noticed in 1880 by Pierre Curie (husband of Marie Curie).

This effect is called piezoelectricity, with piezo- based on the Greek word meaning to press. The minerals quartz and tourmaline both show the piezoelectric effect. This effect is used to produce flashing lights on trainers and other shoes as the wearer walks. Pressure on the crystals separates the positive and negative charge, the charge is used to generate a very small current – enough to light small bulbs.

Low pressure ideas

Sometimes we need to decrease the pressure by increasing the area. Here are some examples.

Pressure is reduced when force is spread over a large surface area.

When you walk on snow you sink in. To prevent this, you can spread out the force over a larger area than your shoes. Skis and snowshoes both do this well. Snowmobiles use caterpillar tracks to increase the area in contact with the soft snow and so reduce the pressure.

Just as snow yields to pressure when walked on, so does the sand in the desert. For this reason, camels have evolved feet with a large surface area, to walk over sand without sinking in.

3 Working with a partner, choose one of the following topics to carry out research on the internet.

- ski designs
- artificial diamonds
- units of pressure
- piezoelectric effect

Record the two best web addresses you find. Prepare an illustrated two-minute talk about your most interesting findings. You can prepare your presentation using PowerPoint.

Building pressure

In very old buildings, the walls were often placed straight on the ground. If a building is large and heavy, and the ground is not hard enough, the pressure may drive the walls into the ground and cause the walls to sink or buckle. This spreads their weight.

Modern houses and offices are built on a thick slab of concrete under the whole building, which gives a strong foundation because it spreads the pressure. Even garden walls are now usually built on a concrete foundation wider than the walls.

4 Some early buildings have no foundations but are built on rock. Why was this a good idea?

Pressure underground

The weight of layers of rock is so great that pressure deep underground is enormous. The effect can be seen in fossils preserved in sedimentary rocks.

Fossils of particular creatures are used by geologists to work out the sequence, and hence the age, of layers of rock. A common fossil which lived in Britain in the early Jurassic period is the ammonite *Psiloceras*. When living, it was an attractive coiled shell with a mother-of-pearl surface but, in being fossilised under tonnes of rock, is found pressed completely flat by the pressure.

Some pressure marks themselves become fossilised. Imagine a dinosaur leaving impressions of its footprints in damp clay. Then over many years sediments fill the footprints and more layers build up. The layers are buried, and heat and enormous underground pressures harden them. Millions of years later, earth movements bring the layers to the surface, the sediments are worn away and the footprints reappear. Careful study of dinosaur footprints can tell us the size and weight of the animal, whether it walked on two legs or four and even how fast it moved.

5 Give two examples of pressure effects in rocks.

Metals are malleable

One of the useful properties of metals is that they are malleable. This means that they can be put under pressure or bent without breaking – they are not brittle.

We use lots of metal in the form of sheets and foils. For example, cars are made from sheet steel and cooking foil is made from aluminium. Both are produced in the same way. A block of the metal, often heated first, is squeezed between rollers of harder metal. As the block goes through the rollers, the enormous pressure makes it thinner. By repeating the rolling process, metal sheets of different thickness are made.

Review

Work in small groups to answer these questions. Prepare to explain your answers to the class.
- Why do camels have broad feet?
- How can you calculate the pressure under your shoes?
- How was flint used in the Stone Age?
- Explain one sport in terms of pressure effects.

Chapter summary

In this chapter you have found out that:
- The same force can produce different pressures according to the area on which the force is applied.
- You can calculate pressure by dividing the force in newtons by the area in square metres.
- Sharp objects such as nails, blades and stakes concentrate the force into a small area, increasing the pressure.
- A force can be spread out over a large area. This reduces the pressure. Snow shoes are an example of this effect.
- Foundations reduce the pressure of buildings on the ground and make it less likely that they will sink.

Pressure in liquids and gases

Introduction

In this chapter we look at how liquids and gases change when they are under pressure.

- Gases can be compressed but liquids cannot.
- Particles in gases and liquids are arranged differently.
- In gases and liquids, pressure acts in all directions.
- In gases and liquids, pressure increases with depth.
- Special technologies are needed when using high pressures.

Weather balloons carry measuring instruments high up into the atmosphere to study the weather. When they are launched, they are half empty, but grow larger as they rise in the atmosphere. Why is this? Hint: The atmosphere is densest at ground level.

Particle pictures

The way particles are arranged in gases and liquids are quite different.

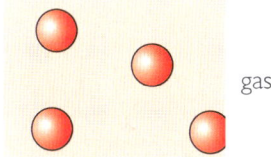
gas

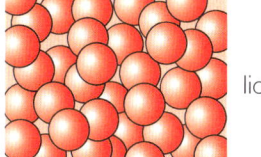
liquid

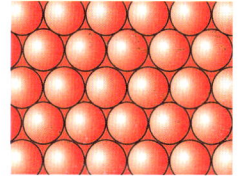
solid

The arrangement of particles in gases, liquids and solids.

In gases there are big spaces between the particles. In both solids and liquids, all the particles are touching other particles. In liquids, the particles can move relative to each other and their arrangement is not regular. The particles in solids are regularly arranged – they are in fixed positions and cannot change neighbours.

1 You are going to do some experiments on compression.

You will need:
- plastic syringe
- water and cooking oil
- safety goggles   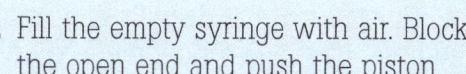 Wear safety goggles.

This is what you do:

1 Fill the empty syringe with air. Block the open end and push the piston
- Can you compress the gas?

2 Repeat using water, then oil, instead of air

3 Explain any differences in compression of the gas and liquids. Use the particle diagrams to help you.

Measuring air pressure

Put an empty glass into water so that it fills up, hold it upside down and then partly lift it out. You will see something odd. With the rim still under water, the water stays inside.

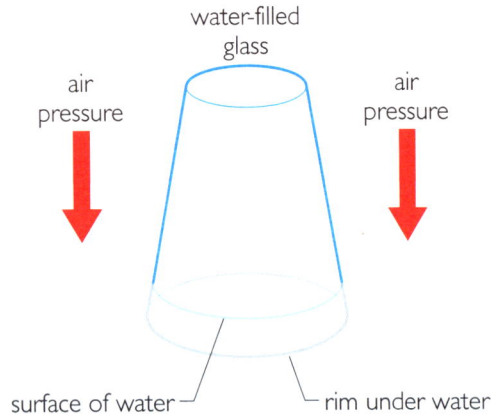

water-filled glass

air pressure

air pressure

surface of water

rim under water

Mysterious empty space

The Italian scientist Evangelista Torricelli (1608–1647) investigated the way liquids stayed inside upturned containers. Instead of water he used a dish of mercury, the dense liquid metal. Torricelli found that he could keep making the glass tube longer and longer, and still the liquid stayed inside the tube, held there by air pressure outside.

Once the tube was about 80 cm long, he noticed something different. At the top of the tube there was an empty space above where the mercury level had settled. The column of mercury inside the tube varied very slightly but was never longer than 76 cm above the level of mercury in the dish. Even when he leaned the tube to one side, the mercury changed to keep the same height of 76 cm above that level. He realised that air pressure was strong enough to support the weight of 76 cm of mercury, and no more.

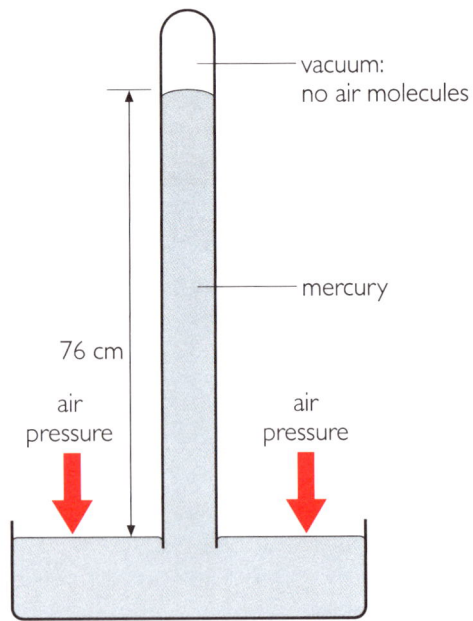

vacuum: no air molecules

mercury

76 cm

air pressure

air pressure

The air pressure exactly balances the weight of the mercury column.

Pressure is force per unit area, and weight is the force due to gravity. So the weight of air per unit area pressing down on the surface of the liquid exactly balanced the weight of mercury in the tube per unit area pressing down on the dish of mercury.

The space above the mercury was empty: Torricelli had created a vacuum. He realised that the column of mercury was an exact measure of the air pressure at that particular time, and with this simple equipment he had invented the barometer.

Air pressure changes slightly from day to day. This means that the height of the mercury column also changes slightly. Higher air pressure supports a higher column of mercury. The weather maps you see on TV show curved lines – isobars – that link places with equal air pressure. The pattern of these isobars gives us information about future changes in the weather. Isobars close together mean the pressure is changing a lot, and that there are strong winds blowing from a high pressure area to one of lower pressure.

Trouble with boiling water

At ground level, water boils at 100 °C. The boiling point of water changes if the surrounding air pressure changes: the higher the air pressure, the higher the boiling point.

At the bottom of a deep mine, you cannot boil water at 100 °C. In the mine, there is more air above you than at the surface, and so the air pressure is higher. At a certain depth, the water boils at 105 °C. We can see a similar effect by using a pressure cooker. The sealed lid makes the pressure inside higher than normal. The boiling point of water is raised and the food cooks faster at this higher temperature.

The opposite effect can be seen at the top of a mountain. On Mont Blanc in the Alps, a kettle would boil at only 85 °C. This is not hot enough to make a good cup of tea or even to boil an egg.

2 In Denver, Colorado, known as the Mile High City, water boils at either 105 °C or 95 °C. Which is correct? How did you work out the right answer?

3 You are going to blow up some books.

You will need:
- several kilos of books
- large plastic bag with a small opening

This is what you do:

1 Spread the bag flat on the table

2 Pile the books on top

3 Blow into the bag and raise the books into the air without touching them at all

- With this arrangement, you can also lift someone sitting on a flat board.

Science at the pool

When you swim underwater you soon notice two things about pressure. No matter which way you turn, the pressure stays the same. Pressure in liquids is the same from all directions. If you dive right down to the bottom of the pool, you notice the increase in pressure on your chest but the pressure increases all over your body. In liquids, the pressure increases with depth. At a depth of only 10 metres, the pressure is doubled! This is why deep-sea divers need diving suits to protect them from the high pressures and allow them to breathe.

Danger for divers

Professional divers who work at great depths must be very careful about how fast they return to the surface. When you open the top of a bottle of lemonade quickly, bubbles appear in the liquid and it starts to froth. The pressure inside the sealed bottle is higher than normal and has been suddenly lowered. In a similar way, if a diver ascends too quickly, the lower pressure causes their blood to froth as bubbles of nitrogen gas appear in it. Bubbles obstruct blood flow in the small blood vessels, and the diver experiences 'the bends' or compressed-air sickness. It is very painful and can be fatal.

The treatment is to put the diver in a decompression chamber. The air pressure is increased to re-dissolve the bubbles in the blood, and is then decreased very slowly so that the level of gases can rebalance naturally. The diver will then recover.

Pressure engineering

Modern aircraft fly very high in the atmosphere where the outside pressure is very low. This is why the passenger cabin is pressurised, to maintain a comfortable air pressure. The pressure in the cabin is usually a bit lower than at ground level, and as the plane descends the cabin pressure is increased towards the normal. If the descent is rapid, passengers often notice pressure effects in their ears as they adjust to the changing air pressure.

Submarines have to cope with the opposite problem. The hull must be strong enough to withstand the enormous pressures outside, while inside the submarine, air pressure must be kept close to normal for the crew. Both aircraft and submarines use the same basic shape, a metal tube with a circular cross-section. This the best shape to withstand large pressure changes. (See page 40.)

4 Give one similarity and one difference in the design of aircraft and submarines.

Submarine stories

This extract is taken from Jules Verne's book *Twenty thousand leagues under the sea*, first published in 1870.

Captain Nemo showed me the full range of his vessel's instruments, from thermometer to manometer, or depth-gauge, and explained to me the locomotive power of the Nautilus. It was gained by electricity.

He went on to explain how the strength of the Nautilus was due to its having two hulls, fitted one inside the other in a cellular arrangement, so that they resisted as if they were a single, immensely thick hull. Not only were these hulls capable of resisting projectiles, but also the unimaginable pressures of the depths to which the vessel could sink by filling its reservoirs. Electricity again drove the pumps which expelled the water and allowed the vessel to rise again. The jets of water, which had earlier been mistaken for the exhalations of some giant cetacean, were the final expulsion of water when the vessel reached the surface.

5 Work with a partner to answer these questions. When you finish, explain your answers to another group.

a What is the purpose of a manometer on the Nautilus?

b Why was the hull strong?

c How did the Nautilus return to the surface?

6 A manometer is an instrument for measuring the pressure of gases and liquids. Work in pairs to make your own manometer.

You will need:
- clear plastic tube about 1 m long
- clamp stands to hold tube in place
- ruler
- small funnel
- water
- salt

This is what you do:

1 Bend and fix the tube vertically in the shape of a letter U

2 Use the funnel to add water until each arm of the U–tube holds about 10 cm water

3 Blow very gently into one arm and mark the positions of the two water levels. The difference in level gives the pressure as centimetres of water

4 Connect the tube to a gas tap, gradually turn the tap full on, then measure the gas pressure in the same way

5 Compare results using other liquids, such as strong salt water which is more dense than tap water.

⚠️ *Care: gas/air mixtures are explosive.*

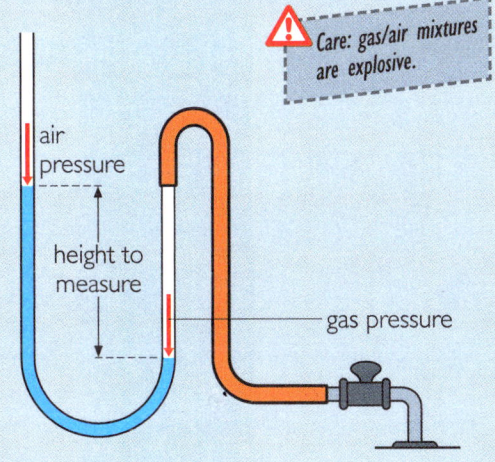

The water manometer.

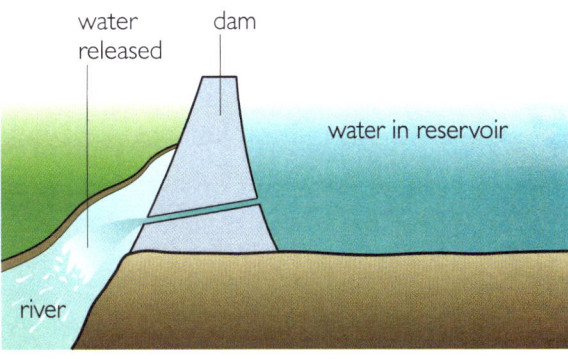

Cross-section through a dam.

7 Explain why the wall of a dam is very thick and wide at the base but much thinner higher up.

Working with high pressures

Cleaning a car can be rather a dull job. But modern high pressure water jets make it easier and quicker. Similarly, water jets are used to clean buildings or pavements.

The pressure inside an aerosol can is quite high. The can contains a gas – the propellant – made liquid by high pressure. This is mixed with the product you want to spray, which can be anything from antiperspirant to car paint. When you press the button, the pressure inside forces the mixture out of the nozzle, and, since the pressure drops inside the can, some of the propellant changes from liquid to gas.

It is dangerous to throw empty aerosol cans on to flames since any remaining gas may expand and explode, sending sharp pieces of metal everywhere.

Some factories operate equipment at pressures of about 400 atmospheres. This is 400 times normal air pressure. If the pipes leak, it can be very dangerous. Stopping water leaking from a damaged pipe is bad enough. Stopping a gas leaking at 400 atmospheres could be a major problem, and so very careful safety precautions are taken.

Review

Work in a small group. Use the particle theory to explain each of the topics below. You will be asked to explain one of your answers to the class.

- The difference between gases and solids.
- Why we cannot compress liquids.
- Why divers may suffer from the bends.

Chapter summary

In this chapter you have found out that:

- Because gases have spaces between particles, gases can be compressed.
- Liquids cannot be compressed since the particles are all in contact with each other.
- In liquids, the pressure increases with depth, but the pressure is the same in all directions at a particular depth. Submarine design takes this into account.
- Aircraft and submarines both have strong circular cross-sections made of metal, to withstand pressure differences.

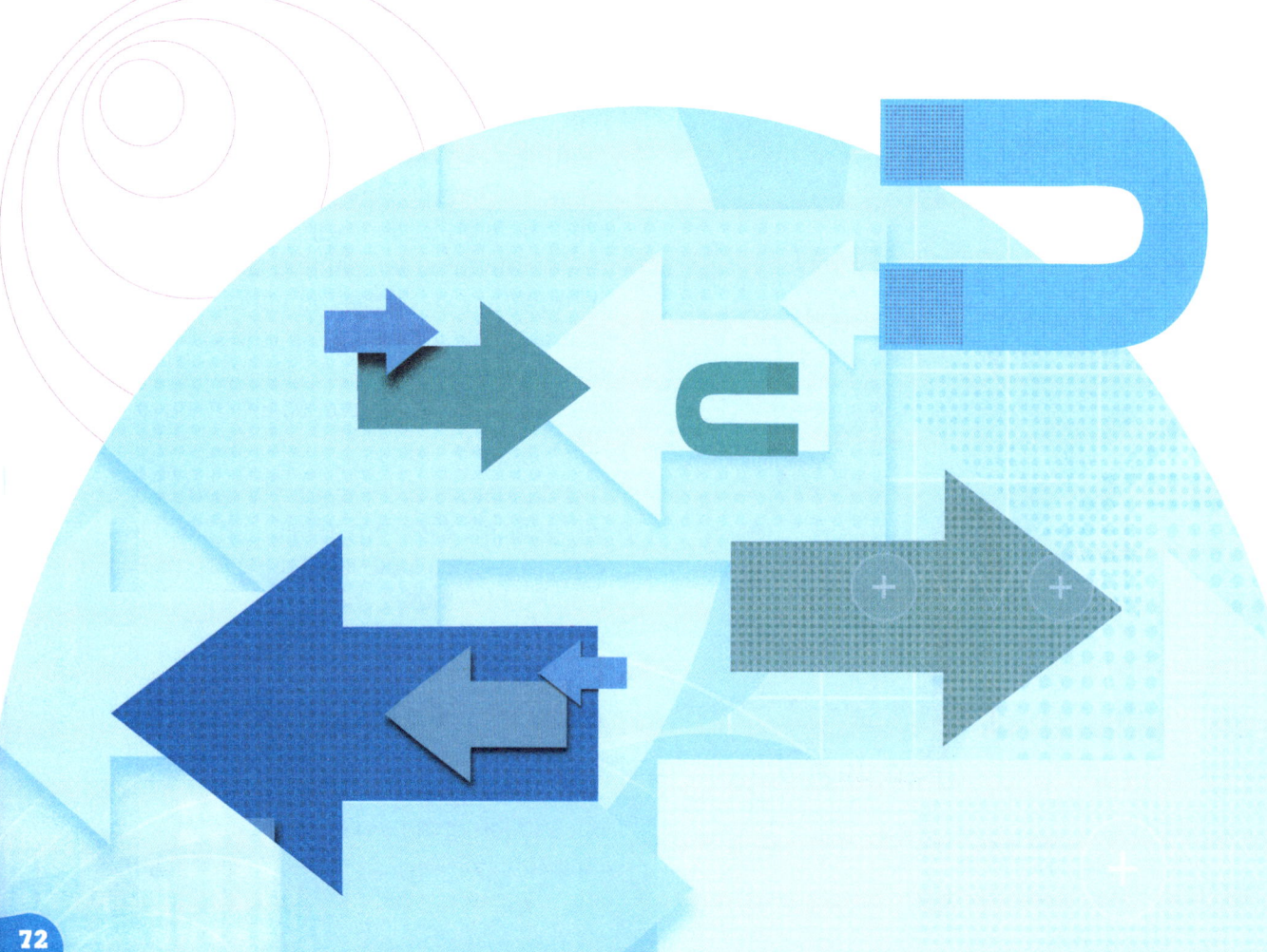

Using pressure

Introduction

In this chapter we look at pneumatics and hydraulics:

- Pneumatics means using gas under pressure.
- Pneumatics has uses in transport, old and new.
- Hydraulics means using liquids under pressure.
- Hydraulics has uses in cars, lifts and in pumping water.

Think of as many words as you can that start with the same letters as the word hydraulics. Are there any connections?

Working with air and steam

The history of pneumatics goes back a long way. The inventor, Hero of Alexandria (around 62AD), developed a steam-powered engine called the aeolipile. It is described in his book called Pneumatica. The engine was simply a metal sphere fitted with two short tubes on opposite sides. When the water inside the sphere was heated, it boiled and the steam poured out of the tubes. The escape of steam produced opposite forces that made the sphere spin around. It was a simple steam engine.

1 If the sphere had one tube only, what might have happened? Explain your answer.

Early bicycles used solid tyres, often made of wood or rubber. A Scottish vet called John Dunlop invented the pneumatic, air-filled, tyre in 1888. His idea was to put pneumatic tyres on his son's bicycle. The first cars fitted with pneumatic tyres were made in 1895, designed in France by the Michelin brothers.

2 What is the advantage of an air-filled car tyre compared with a solid tyre? Explain in terms of particles.

steam

sphere containing
boiling water

Steam jets on opposite sides force the sphere to rotate.

Car tyres used to have a rubber inner tube which was inflated by an air pump, just like bicycle tyres. Modern car tyres are now tubeless. Instead, the air inside the tyre produces enough pressure to seal the tyre edges against the wheel rim.

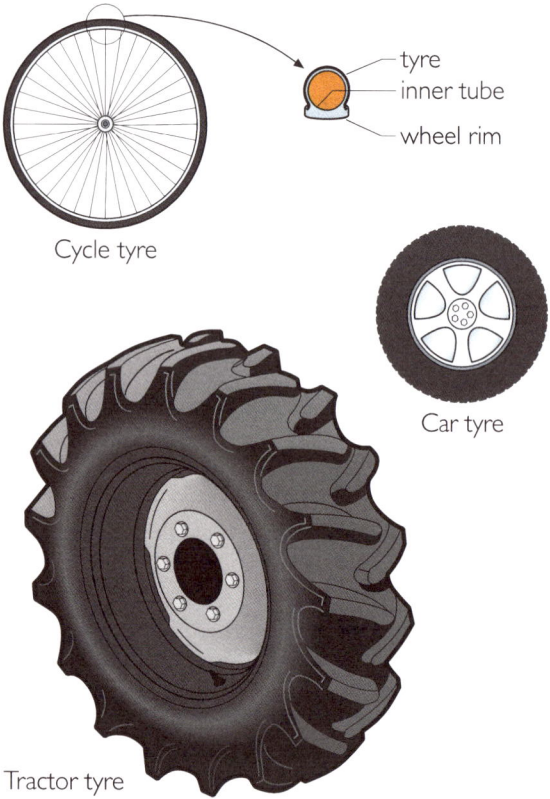

Cycle tyre

tyre
inner tube
wheel rim

Car tyre

Tractor tyre

Different tyre designs.

The pneumatic train

An English engineer called Vallance thought that trains could be designed using pneumatic power. In 1824 he suggested a plan for a pneumatic train from London to Brighton. The idea was to construct a huge tube in which the train would fit. Air would be pumped out ahead of the train, and air pressure behind the train would propel it forwards 'at the speed of a cannon ball'. His plan was never tested, but it could have been faster than today's Channel Tunnel trains if it had worked as Vallance intended.

3 What problems might there be in travelling in a pneumatic train inside a steel pipe?

Until about 20 years ago, the staff in shops such as large department stores used to send money and messages to the cashier's office inside cylinders. They were shot along a system of overhead pipes by air at high pressure.

4 You are going to send some messages using air pressure.

You will need:
- length of clear plastic tubing
- cylinder that just fits inside the plastic tube, e.g. drinking straw or similar
- clay to seal the cylinder ends

This is what you do:

1 Cut a straw to make a short cylinder that just fits inside the plastic tube

2 Write a message on a scrap of paper and put it inside the straw

3 Seal the ends of the cylinder and place it inside the tube

4 Send the message to the other end of the tube by applying air pressure. You can use a plastic syringe, a bicycle pump or blow into the tube

5 The person receiving the message must reply

- Think of one practical use of this pneumatic message system.

Hydraulics

Since the particles in liquids are very close together, you cannot compress liquids. However, unlike solids, liquids can flow. Pressure on a liquid will be transmitted to its container: compressing a balloon of water will transmit the same pressure all round the sides of the balloon.

The study of the flow of liquids and the way they can transmit pressure is called hydraulics. The name comes from two Greek words, *hudor* meaning water and *aulos* meaning a pipe.

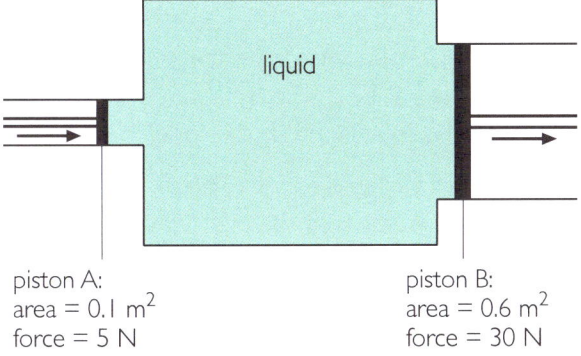

piston A:
area = 0.1 m^2
force = 5 N

piston B:
area = 0.6 m^2
force = 30 N

A small force on piston A develops a large force on piston B.

In hydraulics we use the equation:

$$\text{Pressure} = \frac{\text{force}}{\text{area}}$$

The *pressure* is the same right through the liquid. If piston B is 10 times bigger than piston A:

$$\text{Pressure} = \frac{\text{force}}{\text{area}}$$

$$= \frac{10 \times \text{force}}{10 \times \text{area}}$$

The *force* on the larger piston will be ten times bigger. The small piston moves further than the large one but the force is magnified.

5 A mass of 1 kg is equivalent to a force (weight) of about 10 N. If the ratio of the areas of two pistons is 1:5, work out the force in newtons if a mass of 5 kg is placed on the smaller piston.

Car braking systems

Cars use hydraulics in their braking systems.

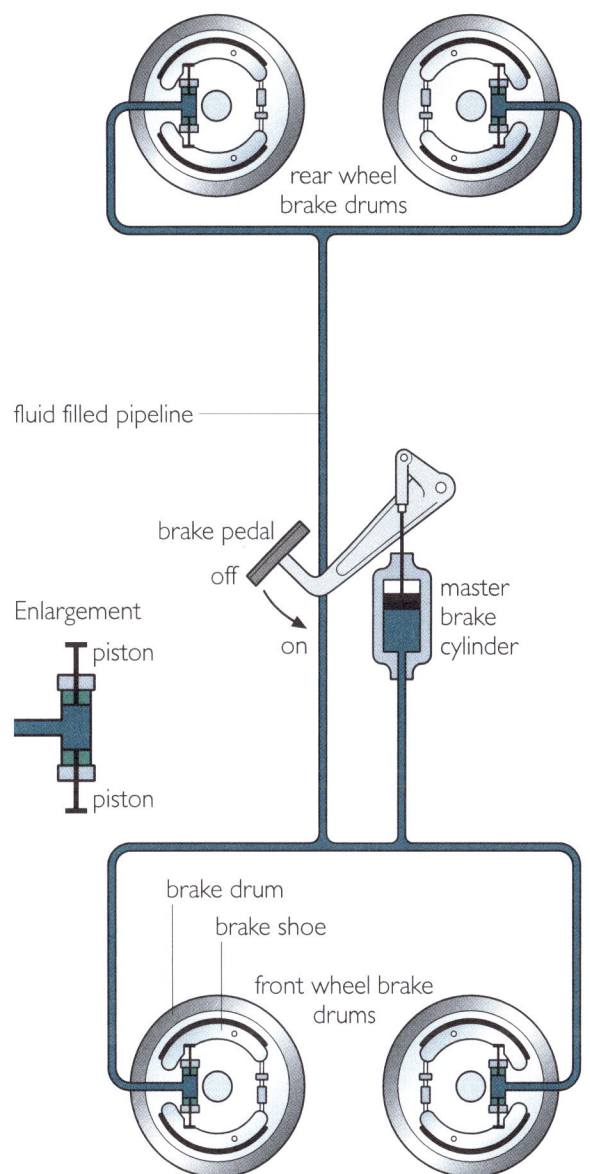

rear wheel brake drums

fluid filled pipeline

brake pedal

off

on

Enlargement

piston

piston

master brake cylinder

brake drum

brake shoe

front wheel brake drums

The braking system of a car. The same branched pipeline reaches all four wheels equally so that the brake fluid transmits the same force to all four wheels.

As the car driver presses down on the brake pedal, the liquid is forced along the pipes to each wheel. The brake shoe is forced against the brake drum, and friction slows the movement of each wheel equally. There will be some frictional heating to the brake shoes and drums as the kinetic energy of the car is turned into heat in the brakes.

6 Why would it be a problem if an air bubble formed in the brake pipe? Explain your answer in terms of particles.

7 You are going to make a model hydraulic lift.

You will need:
- plastic bag fitted with a leak-proof tube about 2 m long
- filter funnel
- water
- pile of books

This is what you do:

1 Spread out the bag and pile some books on top

2 Hold the tube vertically and fix the funnel in the end

3 Pour water down the tube into the bag

4 Observe how the model hydraulic lift raises the books.

8 Working with a partner, choose one of the following topics to carry out research on the internet.
- Hero of Alexandria
- pneumatic tyres
- hydraulic lifts
- disc brakes

Record the two best web addresses you find. Prepare an illustrated 2-minute talk about your most interesting findings. You can make a presentation using PowerPoint.

Water friction

When water is carried through long pipes, there is considerable friction between the water and the sides of the pipe that slows down the flow of water. For this reason, engineers use water pipes that are wider than seems necessary to deliver a given volume of water. There is a very large increase in water flow if the diameter of the pipe is doubled.

For example, let's compare a 5 cm diameter pipe with a 2.5 cm diameter pipe. The cross-sectional area of the larger pipe is only four times bigger than the smaller one. Yet the larger pipe delivers about five times as much water as the smaller one.

Similar effects are seen in rivers: the water flows more slowly at the bottom of a river where friction with the river bed is the greatest. One old science book suggested throwing pieces of turnip into a stream to work out how fast it was flowing! The observer had to time the turnip as it passed between two markers on the river bank.

9 Work with a partner to answer these questions. When you finish, explain your answers to another group.

a Why do water engineers use wider pipes than might be thought necessary to deliver water at a given rate?

b Write notes to explain how you could measure the speed of flow of a river.

c Why doesn't water in a river all flow at the same speed?

Applications of hydraulics

Since hydraulic machines can multiply forces many times, they have lots of useful applications.

- When people first started to make wine from grapes, they had to press the juice from the ripe fruit. This was done by standing inside the container and pressing down the grapes by stamping on them to squeeze out the grape juice. Hydraulic presses are now used to extract juice from grapes and from many other kinds of fruit. They are powerful enough to press oil from seeds, such as olive oil or sunflower oil.

- The hydraulic ram was invented by Montgolfier in 1796, one of the famous brothers who developed hot air balloons. Hydraulic rams force water from a lower to a higher level. A hydraulic ram can be used to move river water up, for example, to a reservoir for later use, or to high parts of a canal, to replace the water that flows down through locks as they are opened.

- When an aircraft comes in to land, you notice a series of noises just before touch down. These are from the hydraulic systems that lower the undercarriage of the aircraft so that the wheels are ready for landing.

- Tractors and bulldozers also use hydraulics to operate the moving parts of their machinery. The high pressure fluid is carried along strong flexible pipes that can be connected easily.

- When lorries collect waste for recycling they use hydraulic lifts to raise the heavy bins and empty them.

- If a car tyre is damaged or punctured, a hydraulic jack can be used to raise the car off the ground. Even a small jack enables a person to raise a car that weighs 1 tonne so that the wheel can be changed.

Ascenseurs

In 1867 the French engineer Leon Edoux developed a hydraulic passenger lift that was called an 'ascenseur'. It used huge pistons to provide the force needed to raise the lift and its passengers. Probably his most famous hydraulic lift was the one he designed in 1889 for the Eiffel Tower in Paris.

Review

Divide the class into four teams, each with a team captain. Each team discusses the questions, with the captain recording the answers.

- How did Hero's steam engine work?
- How did pneumatics make travel more comfortable?
- How does a car brake system work?
- How could you demonstrate the principle of a hydraulic lift?

Chapter summary

In this chapter you have found out that:

- Gas under pressure in car tyres is one example of pneumatics.
- Gas pressure has been used to send messages through pipes.
- Hydraulics allows a small force to be magnified many times.
- Hydraulic systems are used in car brakes, to lower aircraft wheels and in bulldozers.

Answers

Balanced forces
P7 Q2
a Being heavier, larger people exert a greater force and require a large force to move them.
b An extra tugger would unbalance the forces and that team should win.

Mass and weight
P16 Q1
a 278.3 N
b 960.4 N
c 9604 N
P16 Q2
a 178 kg = 1744 N, 317 kg = 3107 N, 442 kg = 4332 N, 635 kg = 6223 N, 216 kg = 2117 N, 89 kg = 872 N, 362 kg = 3548 N
P17 Q3
a 96 N
b 190 800 N
c 10 200 N
d 33.6 N

Gravity extra
P22 Q4
a Held in position by the Sun's gravity.
b 2062 AD
P22 Q5
a As the comet approaches the Sun, the Sun's energy reaching it increases, more ice is vaporised, giving a larger tail.
b The force of the solar wind blows the tail away from the Sun.
P23 Q6
a All bodies orbit the Earth.
b They showed that objects can orbit other bodies, so the geocentric system was wrong.

Science and the Martians
P26 Q1
a Sometimes Mars is stationary, sometimes its movement is retrograde.
b Forwards on days 1-3, retrograde on days 3-4, forwards from day 5 onwards.
c Retrograde movement is seen because the Earth and Mars are both in orbit around the same star, the Sun, with the Earth on the inside orbit.
P28 Q5
a Age at their next birthday plus four and a half years.
b It is easier from Mars, the planet has less mass than the Earth and so its gravity is weaker than Earth's.
c Mass is the amount of substance, not a force, so it would be the same.

Friction
P31 Q2
a Kinetic energy of motion is converted into heat by friction.
b Frictional heating may be enough to ignite the sawdust.

Streamlining
P37 Q1
Cars now have a low profile, they are enclosed and have a smooth shape (any two).
P37 Q3
a As train speeds have increased, air resistance has become more of a problem and drag had to be reduced.
b Coaches have smooth windows and doors and no gaps between coaches, giving a streamlined shape.
c Trains might become unstable and leave the rails; air resistance is greater at ground level.

Magnetic attraction
P43 Q1
Drawing shows new N and S poles at the cut edge; poles are in pairs, N and S on each new magnet.
P44 Q4
a iron
b Use a magnet, the filings stick to the magnet but the sand does not.
c Aluminium is not magnetic.
P44 Q5
Yes; this is why fridge magnets stick in place.
P45 Q7
a Train and track need to have the repulsion of like poles to raise the train above the track.
b Opposite poles would attract and the train would stick in one place.
P45 Q9
The train needs to have like poles for all the couplings: they would always repel and never join up.

Magnetic fields
P48 Q1
a north-south direction
b The bars became magnetic.
c No, the rotation of the Earth may not be connected to its magnetic field at all.
P49 Q4
The end of the compass is a magnetic south pole since opposite poles attract.

Electromagnets
P54 Q4
The car is made of steel (iron), a magnetic material, but the tyre is made of non-magnetic rubber.
P55 Q6
a With the high current, long wires would overheat and might melt or the insulation might catch fire.
b a relay switch
P56 Q7
It would be dangerous if acid spilled from the battery since acids are often corrosive.

On the turn
P60 Q3
a Clockwise moment 125 N cm;
anticlockwise moment 125 N cm.
b Clockwise moment 180 N cm;
anticlockwise moment 160 N cm.
c Clockwise moment 120 N cm;
anticlockwise moment 120 N cm.
Seesaws a and c are in balance.
P61 Q7
Go to the Moon since it has weaker gravity and the ball
will travel further before falling back to the ground.

Under pressure
P64 Q1
There is greater pressure under the four table legs than
under the chest's larger flat base which spreads out the
force.
P65 Q4
Rock acts as a strong foundation and spreads the weight
of the walls, reducing the danger of sinking (subsidence).
P65 Q5
Examples include fossil footprints and squashed fossils.

Pressure in liquids and gases
P69 Q2
The name Mile High City indicates that the air pressure is
lower than normal and so the boiling point is lower; it is
95°.
P70 Q4
Both aircraft and submarines have strong near-circular
cross-sections. Aircraft maintain a higher pressure inside
than outside, submarines are the opposite.

P70 Q5
a The manometer acted as a depth gauge for the
submarine.
b There were two hulls, one fitted inside the other.
c Electric pumps removed water from the reservoirs,
replacing it with air, so making Nautilus lighter.

Using pressure
P73 Q1
Instead of spinning round, the sphere could have moved
in one direction like a rocket, away from the escaping
steam.
P73 Q2
The air-filled tyre absorbs bumps in the road giving a
smoother ride.
P74 Q3
A leak would stop the train; it would be impossible to get
out; there would be problems with ventilation; there were
no windows.
P75 Q5
Ratio is 1:5, so it is 5 kg:25 kg, so if 1 kg = 10 N, this gives
25 kg = 250 N.
P76 Q6
Gases have spaces between the particles. When the
brakes are pressed, the gas would compress rather than
passing on the force to the brakes. The brakes would not
go on.
P76 Q9
a Friction between water and the sides of the pipe
reduces the flow rate of the water.
c Friction at the river bed and with the banks slows down
the water.

Index and glossary

7 **equilibrium** a word to describe forces that are in balance

53 **electromagnet** a magnet that is produced by electricity flowing through a coil; it can be switched on and off

44 **ferrite** a ceramic material that is magnetic, used to make fridge magnets

39 **flammable** describes a material that can burn

36 **fluid** a liquid or a gas such as water or air

2 **forces** pushes or pulls

65 **foundation** the strong platform, often made of concrete, used to support a wall or building

30 **friction** a contact force that resists movement and wears things down

32 **frictional heating** caused when the kinetic energy of motion is turned into heat

40 **fuel consumption** the amount of fuel used by a car for a journey

58 **fulcrum** is another word for a pivot, a balance point

23 **Galileo** the Italian astronomer who first observed the moons of Jupiter

23 **geocentric** the model of the Sun and planets that said the Earth was at the centre

47 **geodynamo** the system of electrically conducting material in the Earth's interior that circulates and produces the Earth's magnetic field

46 **geologist** a scientist who studies rocks and fossils

42 **Gilbert, William** the Elizabethan scientist who first realised that the Earth itself was a magnet

49 **GPS** global positioning system, which gives your position using signals from satellites

33 **graphite** a form of carbon used as a lubricant and to make the 'lead' of pencils

19 **gravity** the force that attracts all objects to all other objects, however big or small

22 **Halley, Edmond** the astronomer after whom Halley's comet is named

63 **hallmark** the standard mark used on silver and gold objects to guarantee their purity

31 **heavy spar** the mineral (barium sulphate) used in drilling mud

39 **helium** the unreactive gas used in modern airships and in party balloons

5 **Hooke's law** the law that says the extension of a spring is proportional to the load on it

75 **hydraulics** the study of the flow of liquids and the way they can transmit pressure

77 **hydraulic ram** a type of pump used to move water, invented in 1796

39 **hydrodynamic drag** the friction experienced when something moves through water

39 **hydrogen** the lightest gas; the commonest element in the universe

38 **Icarus** son of Daedulus who in myth fell to his death when his wings melted

33 **ice yacht** a winter-sports yacht that slides on runners over the ice

10 **inertia** the tendency of objects to stay in one place and resist movement

4 **inflation system** blows up car airbags in a crash

68 **isobars** lines on a weather map that link areas of equal air pressure

10 **laws of motion** the laws developed by Isaac Newton to describe motion

8 **leaning tower of Pisa** tower in Italy whose foundations began to sink on one side during construction

57 **lever** a bar that turns about a pivot, such as a bottle opener or crowbar

45 **levitation** floating above a surface without any physical contact

48 **lines of force** show the shape of the magnetic field around a magnet

42 **lodestone** the magnetic mineral now known as magnetite, an iron oxide

33 **lubricant** a material that reduces friction between surfaces such as graphite or engine oil

45 **maglev** a type of train that uses magnetic levitation to reduce friction

47 **magnetic field** the volume around a magnet where you can detect its magnetism

42 **magnetite** the mineral in lodestone, magnetic iron oxide

66 **malleable** able to bend without breaking; a property of metals

70 **manometer** a device that measures pressure by the difference in levels of liquid

25 **Mars** the red planet and also the Roman god of war

15 **mass** the amount of material in something

68 **mercury** the liquid metal, used in some thermometers

28 **methane** one of the gases in natural gas; a hydrocarbon containing only hydrogen and carbon atoms

20 **meteors, meteorites** small fragments of rock in space are meteors, but if they reach the Earth's surface they are called meteorites

20 **Moon** the Earth's natural satellite; many planets have their own moons

10 **Newton, Isaac** the scientist who developed the laws of motion

5 **newtonmeter** a device for measuring forces

5 **newton** the unit of force

29 **Olympus Mons** the largest known volcano in the Solar System, on the planet Mars; it is extinct

25 **opposition** the arrangement of the Sun, Earth and Mars all in a line, with the Earth in the middle

27 **ozone** the gas in the upper atmosphere that protects life from too much ultraviolet radiation from the Sun

46 **palaeomagnetism** the magnetism in ancient rocks

21 **Piazzi, Giuseppe** discoverer of the first asteroid

64 **piezoelectricity** electricity produced by applying pressure to some kinds of crystals

57 **pivot** or fulcrum, the turning point of a force

28 **planetary swing-by** the use of a planet's gravity to propel a spacecraft on its journey

73 **pneumatics** means using gas under pressure

42 **poles** the ends of a magnet or the geographical and magnetic poles of the Earth

62 **pressure** force per unit area

71 **propellant** the material that produces pressure in an aerosol can

13 **reaction** the opposite to the action of a force: if you pull an object, it pulls back

13 **recoil** the force in the opposite direction to a bullet leaving a gun

55 **relay** a double circuit where a small current in one circuit switches on a large current in another one

26 **retrograde motion** the apparent backwards movement of Mars in the sky

43 **rules of magnetism** that like poles repel but unlike poles attract

27 **Schiaparelli, Giovanni** Italian astronomer who saw marks on the surface of Mars

11 **seat-belt** a safety device fitted to cars to reduce injuries in crashes

12 **second law of Newton** deals with what happens when a force acts on an object

59 **seesaw** a fun example of the turning effects of forces

4 **sensor** a device that detects a change in something such as temperature or pressure

21 **shooting star** a meteor that glows brightly as it falls towards Earth

17 **Solar System** the Sun and all the planets and other bodies orbiting round the Sun

22 **solar wind** stream of particles from the Sun

53 **solenoid** a coil of wire that carries an electric current

5 **spring balance** a weighing device that uses the extension of a spring for measurements

40 **streamline** describes the smooth shape of an object that reduces friction as it moves through a fluid such as water or air

40 **submarine** a reinforced ship that can operate at great depths under the sea

8 **suspension bridge** a bridge that is supported by cables that hold up the roadway

33 **tribology** the study of how to reduce the effects of friction

7 **tug-of-war** a game where two teams pull on a rope in opposite directions

40 **turbulence** a stirring movement that can be reduced by streamlining

27 **UV** ultraviolet radiation; part of the electromagnetic spectrum; it can be dangerous to health and cause skin cancer

68 **vacuum** a volume containing no particles; outer space is an almost perfect vacuum

36 **velodrome** an indoor cycle track

27 **Viking** the name given to a series of American spacecraft including some to Mars

15 **weight** the force of gravity pulling an object towards the Earth, or another body, weight differs on different planets, while mass stays the same

Published by Letts Educational
The Chiswick Centre
414 Chiswick High Road
London W4 5TF
Telephone: 020 89963333
Fax: 020 87428390
E-mail: mail@lettsed.co.uk
Website: www.letts-education.com

Letts Educational is a division of Granada Learning, part of ITV plc.

ISBN 1 84419 028 5

British Library Cataloguing in Publication Data
A catalogue record for this book is available from the British Library.

Produced by Hart McLeod, Cambridge
Commissioned by Helen Clark
Project management by Julia Swales
Editing by Pat Winter
Design by Bigtop Design, Bicester
Illustrations by Jeff Edwards and Ken Vail Graphic Design
Production by PDQ
Printed and bound in Italy

Acknowledgements
The publishers would like to thank the following for permission to use copyright material. Every effort has been made to trace copyright holders and to obtain their permission for the use of copyright material. The author and publishers will gladly receive information enabling them to rectify any error or omission in subsequent editions.

Photographs: p.3 ©Tim Wright/Corbis; p.15 © Lawrence Manning/Corbis; p.20 © NASA/Roger Ressmeyer/Corbis; p.21©Charles & Josette Lenars/ Corbis; p.22 ©Dennis di Cicco/Corbis; p.25 ©NASA /Roger Ressmeyer/Corbis; p.27 ©Detlev Van Ravenswaay/Science Photo Library; p.31 ©Lowell Georgia/Corbis; p.32 ©Duomo/Corbis; p.33 ©Nils Jorgensen/Rex Features; p.34 ©Rochaphoto/Alamy; p.36 ©John Pierce/Rex Features; p.37 top ©Hulton-Deutsch Collection/Corbis, bottom ©Tim Bird/Corbis; p.39 ©Thierry Orban/Corbis; p.43 ©Richard Megna/Fundamental/Science Photo Library; p.49 ©Yoav Levy/PHOTOTAKE Inc./Alamy; p.50 ©Chase Swift/Corbis; p.54 ©Jeremy Walker/Science Photo Library

Text: p.7 On the Pull (Pimms, stilettos and muscular ministers), by Ros Taylor, ©Guardian Newspapers Ltd 2003; p.16 The World's heaviest man, Guinness Book of Records, ©Random House Inc